POLITICAL
Theory &
SOCIETAL
Ethics

POLITICAL Theory & SOCIETAL Ethics

ROBERT R. CHAMBERS

Prometheus Books • Buffalo, New York

Published 1992 by Prometheus Books

96 95 94 93 92   5 4 3 2 1

Library of Congress Cataloging-in-Publication Data

Chambers, Robert R.
    Political theory and societal ethics / by Robert R. Chambers.
        p.   cm.
    ISBN 0-87975-696-9 (acid-free)
    1. Political ethics. 2. Social ethics. 3. Political science. I. Title.
JA79.C48   1992
172—dc20   91-20513
                                                                CIP

Printed in the United States of America on acid-free paper.

Preface

Joe is dying of cancer and failing rapidly. His golfing buddies, over a beer at the club, recall the things that Joe has done for them. Joe had lent one of them enough money to save his now-prosperous business from going under during a recession. Joe was responsible for reconciling another of the group with his wife, now loved so dearly, when they had veered to the edge of a divorce. The third man was saved by Joe from drowning when a sailboat capsized in the bay. Gratitude, they agree, obligates each of them to do something of appropriate magnitude. They go their respective ways with high moral purpose.

In the next week one of them buys an annuity that is generously adequate to care for Joe's mentally handicapped granddaughter for the rest of her life. Another endows, in Joe's name, a chair of oncology at the local college of medicine. The third one, a writer, suspends all his projects and embarks on Joe's biography.

During the next week, Joe's last on this earth, each of his buddies visits to say goodbye and pledge an irrevocable commitment to his particular course of action. Joe can do little but express sincere gratitude to friends who would make such sacrifices.

Unfortunately, Joe has already provided for the granddaughter and suspects that the additional annuity will merely go to line the pockets of the lawyer and trustee. Privately, Joe blames the medical school for his present state of health and has written bitter letters recommending that the school drop its miserable oncology department. Joe remembers with a shudder the writer inadvertently mangling the reputations of his previous biographees.

Discharging a moral duty does not necessarily produce good results. The actions of his buddies did not produce the benefits they envisioned for Joe.

Moral duties are imposed on individuals and generally require actions that are presumed to be beneficial to their fellow human beings. However, moral duties do not require a beneficial result, and coordination between the people involved to make sure that discharging the duty produces benefits is not usually part of the system of morality. Neither are moral duties conditioned on the outcome of the coordination. Thus, the technique of getting people to do good things by means of moral duties would not seem, on the face of it, to be particularly well-suited for situations in which the making of choices necessarily requires coordination.

And yet morality is the hallmark of value in social processes such as politics, the heart of which is coordination of people's actions through a set of rules or laws. This may be because moral principles are very deeply ingrained and people use them for guidance in any field where they seem to be applicable, as though there were no alternative.

I suggest here that there is an alternative, one that is more appropriate than the technique of moral duties in fields that call for people to coordinate their obligations with each other. Furthermore, the appropriate ethical principles depend on the type of coordination that is involved.

Contents

8   Contents

1

A State of Nature

It was a beautiful summer day, a bit over a hundred and fifty years ago, in a remote corner of the Pacific Ocean that had not yet been affected by Western culture. In this favored place, about fifteen hundred miles west of Chile, lay a splendid chain of three islands. Though missing from the maps of the time, these islands were known to the sailors who happened across them and were called the Tidy Isles. Individually, north to south, the islands went by the names Ajax, Babo, and Comet. Each island lay out of sight, just over the horizon, from the next.

Each island was surrounded by iridescent lagoons and stretches of white-sand beach. On each the coconut palms swayed gently on the shore, like Polynesian dancers, keeping time with the waves. The screeching of parrots flying back and forth through the nearby jungle provided a pleasantly discordant note, an accent to the overall harmony. In the center of each island, around the summit of a tall, steep mountain of black volcanic rock, hung a modest but useful cloud from which came gentle misty rain. And on each island a glorious rainbow hovered over the valleys below.

An observer might well have concluded that these islands were perfect and, like everything perfect, were doomed to decay. And overshadowing that beautiful day the observer might have had a sense of foreboding. Was the natural paradise on these islands soon to disappear, to be remembered, if at all, as a fleeting fantasy? Civilization, in two of its manifold guises, was sailing relentlessly toward the Tidy Isles. Its harbinger was Henry, a humble maverick sailor aboard a bold three-masted ship, the *Caroline,* being wafted north by the gentle breeze sweeping o'er the azure sea.

In command of the *Caroline* was Captain Horace, sitting aft in a small cabin below deck, scratching diligently with his quill pen, making endless entries in the ship's log. He looked up. The noise on the deck above was as familiar as it was disturbing. He heaved a sigh. Soon the first mate would be knocking on his door, insisting again that they discuss Henry.

High up in the rigging, a group of sailors busily trimmed the sails, running up and down the ratlines. Others below swabbed the deck under the benevolent eye of the mate. The sailors and the mate glanced at each other, embarrassed, trying to ignore the aft deck, site of a humiliating scene being acted out by Henry and the bosun. Normally, the sailors' sympathies would have been with one of their own. But they had seen this all before. They knew that Henry had been getting away with too much. Their patience with him was gone.

Of medium height, Henry was slightly built, agile, a bit hyperactive. He had watery blue eyes, sandy blond hair, and a flat face with a perpetually inquisitive expression. Henry shifted warily to one side as the bosun approached, a belaying pin in his fist, intent on herding Henry into a corner.

The bosun, arms outstretched, was a huge and beefy man with a bulldog face. He drooled a little from the corner of his mouth as he leaned forward, brandishing his club, taking short steps on widespread legs. "Get aloft," he growled as he came up close. "Get to work before I beat you to a pulp."

"I don't approve of the way you're running this ship," said Henry in a thin voice while backing away, "and I refuse to participate." The bosun lunged with an angry snarl and swung the pin at Henry's head. Henry ducked, slithered out of the way, and jumped up onto a shroud, scampering up the ratlines just out of the bosun's reach.

"Get on up there where you belong," roared the bosun, "and get the hell to work." He glared up at Henry and bared his teeth. Henry laughed and stuck out his tongue. The bosun's world stood still. His mind went scarlet blank. He trembled with rage and the deck shook. The ship sailed on, ploughing through the waves; the kindly sun shone down on all the company. Sailors, glancing over as they worked, shook their heads. One of them started a chant. Relieved, the rest hurriedly joined in.

"Aargh," screamed the bosun, jumping around onto the ratlines, heaving himself up a few steps toward Henry. But Henry had already swung beneath the ropes and was dropping lightly to the deck. Their positions reversed, Henry looked up and smiled. The bosun, beads of sweat on his brow, peered down at Henry through the ropes.

The bosun hesitated. Nothing he did in these confrontations with Henry worked out the way he intended. The problem with Henry was getting worse. The bosun reflected with anguish that again he must look the fool. Resentment of captain and mate, who'd done little to support him, welled up in his throat till he thought he would choke.

Suddenly, the bosun leaned to the right and drew back his arm. Henry danced two steps away and rose on the balls of his feet. The bosun's arm snapped forward. The belaying pin shot at Henry, who jerked back barely in time. The pin hit a cleat in the deck, jumped high, and cartwheeled over the railing down into the sea.

The bosun banged his face against the ropes and uttered a piteous sob. "Look what you did, you son of a bitch. My pay'll be docked the cost of the pin." He gazed down with a tear in each eye. "Henry, why do you do this to me? Why don't you do what you're supposed to, like everybody else?"

Warily, Henry averted his face and watched from the corner of his eye. "Why should I?"

The bosun, frustrated, sagged forward against the ropes. "Henry, that's what you joined for; that's what you get paid for."

"Ha!" said Henry. "You shanghaied me. And besides, you don't pay me enough to work in your stupid organization."

The ship leaned as it swung around and started the course anew. The breeze blew more briskly. The sun grew hotter. For a long moment the two were motionless. Finally the bosun spoke sadly, "Be reasonable, Henry. How much do you think you're worth?"

"It's just not fair," said the mate. "Bosun chased Henry all over the ship. By the time he gave up, they were both too tired to do any work. Why do you keep me from giving the bosun some help? He's flouting your authority. The men don't like Henry, but sooner or later it's going to destroy their morale."

The captain leaned back in his chair and looked around the cabin. "Me, keep you from doing your job? Now don't you tell me that. It's surprised I am that you haven't yet learned the proper way to handle a simple management problem. I guess I must give you another hint. Suppose you provide the bosun with some help and he catches Henry? Three times already you've given Henry a lashing, and from what you tell me, it's only made him worse. You know you can't let bosun give him a real beating. For sure you wouldn't get work out of him then. And you might tie up another man nursing him back to health."

The mate frowned. "That's not what I had in mind. Next time I'm going to keelhaul him and maybe he'll drown before he makes it up the other side."

The captain curled his lip in reproof. "You ought to know that's something I could never let you do. What would happen if the clerks in London heard? We'd spend years with solicitors, barristers, administrative hearings, depositions, discovery proceedings, and appeals. In fact, that's got to be the stupidest thing you've said yet." His eyes fixed on the mate; he leaned forward, elbows on the table, hands locked together like a tent. "I know Henry makes discipline difficult and I sympathize with your predicament. You can't just throw him in the brig. He'd sit in there idle and laugh." The captain paused and then spoke in a tone welling with sincerity. "I intend this problem to be a test of the executive ability you will need if you ever, by chance, aspire to a promotion."

The mate stared a moment in thought. Then he leaned forward with a sly look. "Aren't we getting close to Comet Island? My recollection is we'll see it tomorrow."

Henry stood in the dinghy waving his fist at the ship, which was rapidly pulling away. "You're marooning me. You have no right," he yelled at the top of his lungs. But the ship moved on. A sailor high in the rigging waved a cheery goodbye.

Henry sat down, tears coming to his eyes, an ache in his gut. He had never gotten along with bosses anywhere or fitted into their organizations. But here, at least, the sailors were his comrades, men he thought were his friends. In retrospect, he could see that they had just been making empty speeches of support. Just minutes ago, they had shown themselves only too happy to grab him and throw him off the ship. He couldn't erase from his memory the gloating looks on their faces as they shoved him into the little boat and pushed it away.

He wiped his eyes, snuffled, and looked at the island. It seemed big, miles of shoreline. Was it inhabited? Would the people be friendly? Suppose they were cannibals? How could he ingratiate himself? Henry sat there in the boat as the waves rocked it gently. Finally a sense of anticipation crept over him. The idea of being marooned on a nice big island smacked of adventure. He scanned the shore slowly from left to right and saw no sign of human habitation. He was looking into the sun so this must be the south end of the island. Directly ahead of him was a natural harbor. He picked up the oars and rowed toward shore.

Henry jumped out onto the beach and dragged his dinghy across the sand above the high-tide mark. He emptied out the things they had left him and looked around. There were bushes in the sand dunes at the back of the beach. He dragged the little boat over and pushed it under a large, dense bush. Then he pulled up a leafy little bush and swept out his tracks.

He sorted out his belongings. There wasn't much: his bag of clothing and personal effects, a musket with powder and twenty balls, a knife, a rusty old ax, a flint and steel, some moldy biscuits, water, and a piece of canvas for shelter. What was the next step? Henry had to find out what the island was like and he didn't dare leave any of this behind. He loaded the musket, tucked the knife in his belt, and rolled everything else up in the canvas. Hoisting the roll on one shoulder and the musket on the other, he set off up the shore.

Two weeks later, his trip completed, Henry stood alongside the dinghy again. He'd been around the whole of the island and found no sign of other people. The island was his alone. He felt exhilarated. Putting his load down, he danced a jig. His personal island was a fertile land with streams of fresh water, all types of food, and many places to build a home. He hadn't eaten the biscuits; there had been plenty of fruits, vegetables, and fish in the streams. He had shot and cooked a wild pig the seventh day out, the gastronomical high point of the trip.

As he expected, the dinghy was untouched. He dragged it back to the water, loaded his duffel, launched the dinghy, and rowed a half day's walk up the eastern shore where he had decided to settle. Landing, he carried everything up to a pleasant grove of trees and put it down. Nearby was a good-sized stream of fresh water. He had explored the stream and found that it ran down from the mountain through the jungle onto a big meadow, then through groves of trees and down into a marsh by the ocean. The marsh was an important factor in his selection. He'd found there an abundance of both fish and shellfish.

The next few months, busy night and day, Henry worked happily, singing to himself. Diligent and energetic, he jumped up at the crack of dawn, worked all day to build his home and farm, and then did handicrafts by the light of his fire in the evening. He built a rock-wall enclosure for defense, a hut to sleep in, food storage sheds, and fireplaces inside and out. He made furniture, utensils, tools, clothing, and sandals. He planted a garden and a grove of fruit trees.

Finally, his immediate needs satisfied, Henry began to relax. Living was easy: the weather was nice and the island was rich in resources. His daily chores left him with time to spare. After another month he became restless and, during the next six months, he explored the island again, slowly, area by area. It amazed him that nobody else had settled there yet. Perhaps it was too far off the beaten path. By now he felt quite possessive. The idea of additional settlers was distasteful.

Henry's only real rivals on the island were some large wildcats which he encountered from time to time. They recognized him as a danger, were wary, and he, too, felt no desire to provoke a fight. The relationship soon settled down to one of mutual respect and avoidance. When they did happen to meet, a wildcat and Henry walked carefully around each other and neither interfered with the other's kills.

A year passed. Henry became bored. All this was fine, but it was time for him to get back to civilization. He built an observation post up on the side of the mountain so he could see far out on the ocean. For a while, Henry spent most of his time there keeping an eye out for ships, ready to run down and light the series of bonfires he'd laid for a smoke signal SOS.

Alas, in several months of watching, Henry saw no ships. He became discouraged. Then it occurred to him that getting back to civilization might not be so wonderful after all. It would no doubt mean more bosses, more run-ins with authority, more pressure on him to conform. While he liked people, he preferred those who, like himself, left others alone unless they invited contact. Frankly, he could think of no place where most people behaved that way. This brought on serious reservations about being rescued. He finally decided he would have to refuse any such offer.

Once he abandoned the watch for ships, Henry faced again the problem of what to do with the rest of his life. He was thinking of this as he sat in the meadow, his back to a rock, watching a herd of deer. There must be a better way to live, he thought.

Henry stretched his arms and the herd of deer froze; but turning to look at him, seeing nothing of concern, they went back to grazing. One of the wildcats was on the other side of the deer and took that moment to charge out toward a fawn. The herd took startled jumps and ran off to the other end of the meadow. But the fawn started too late. The wildcat killed it and, crouching there beside its body, peered over at Henry, who shook his head sadly and looked off in another direction.

As the wildcat ate, Henry mulled things over, reviewing the problems he had solved. They had been the practical everyday problems of getting food, shelter, and clothing. By now living was easy. But spending his life doing daily chores was not going to satisfy him. What about the higher things in life? Perhaps he should carve a flute and teach himself to play, or take up painting. Maybe he should start writing a journal and record his experiences.

How would he know what was the best thing to do, the best way to live his life? Henry grappled with the problem until it seemed as pliable as a pillow: whenever he made progress over here it bulged out at him over there. After several episodes of this low-grade ratiocination, he decided that the principal thing he had learned was that he enjoyed the mental exercise.

Though Henry was not aware of it, his life on the island was soon to change. His story—the insubordinate attitude and subsequent marooning—had spread along the waterfront in more than one of the Pacific ports as the *Caroline* made her rounds. Henry wasn't the only sailor viewed as being uncooperative or defiant. For a few drinks Captain Horace was more than willing to tell of his innovative and humanitarian solution to such problems.

"Now, I wouldn't put anybody dangerous in a place like that," he would say, as the other captains nodded in agreement.

The notion of an island full of loners appealed to their sense of humor. "That kind deserves each other," they said, as they left the tavern and staggered down the street. Some of them remembered.

One day, on a hike far from home, Henry saw a hut that looked almost like a copy of his. He loaded his musket and crept silently toward it. Suddenly a deep-voiced challenge rang out. Henry darted behind a tree. A tall, thin man with a booming laugh, a sailor by the look of him, stepped out from behind some bushes and held up his empty hands.

"Peace! My name is Hugh," he said.

Henry put his musket on the ground and reciprocated the gesture. The two met, sat down, and talked while sipping the juice of some fruits that Hugh had picked. Hugh had also been marooned, but had been told that someone was already on the island. He'd found Henry's site, watched him for some time, and then copied his hut far away on the other side of the island. An engineer by nature, Hugh had incorporated a few improvements, which he was pleased to show Henry. Nevertheless, Hugh indicated he had no interest in being social. In fact, he let Henry know that he would have been perfectly happy to live alone without introducing himself. The island was obviously big enough for both of them. As Henry left, each amiably expressed the intention of staying out of the other's way.

The next year, four more ships came by and each marooned a man on the island. The north end, in fact, was becoming known in the trade as Insubordination Beach.

There was room on the island and enough resources to support all six men quite well. Each built a hut away from the rest and lived by himself. Like Henry, the others were not inclined to be aggressive—live and let live was their motto—but each wanted to make sure that nobody else would try to tell him what to do.

Henry found that one of the new settlers, Seymour, shared his fondness for chess, so it wasn't long before they fell into a routine of meeting every week for a few games. As the months wore on, the men began to do a little trading with one another. They did each other favors as needed from time to time if they felt like it. All but Hugh cooperated to build a bridge over the largest stream. When it was done, they all said good-bye and each returned to his own hut to live by himself.

Henry still thought about the question of how best to spend the rest of his life, but the settling of other men on the island had changed the environment and no doubt the answer. Mostly, he noticed that having neighbors improved things for him. He remained free to live his life as before, without interference, as long as he kept to a reasonable area and didn't encroach on someone else. Rather than being a problem, the presence of the other men gave him access to foods and handicrafts by trading and joint activities. They even bolstered his feeling of security inasmuch as an attack by an outsider on one of them would most likely be viewed as an attack on all. In brief, having them around increased the range of things he wanted to do, and made new skills and resources available.

As a group, the sailors got along well because no one intruded on anyone else without permission. As one of them pointed out, it was a golden-rule existence. Each left the others alone because that was what he wanted, too. They neither had nor needed an agreement about this. All of them could see that it worked.

But Henry worried. What if the next sailor were not willing to live that way?

2

Ethics

ETHICS AND MORALITY

Living can be viewed as a succession of choices made and actions taken. Choices are influenced by pains and drives, emotions, perceptions, and conceptual thoughts, and often by several of these at once. One of these overshadows the rest, we make the choice, and in an operational sense this evidently reflects what we think is the best thing to do at that moment. Perhaps few of our choices reflect a considered opinion of what would be best in a formal, long-range sense, but even the trivial chocolate-versus-vanilla choices show what we think will best satisfy our taste, at an instant when we have decided that satisfying our taste is the best thing to do now.

Henry, living alone on Comet Island, constantly made choices, which, according to his lights, were the best choices. But Henry had a reflective turn of mind, and devoted some thought to longer-range problems, to improving his choices in order to lead the best life he could. He thought that the more he could define the best life and the more he could learn about how to reach it, the better his choices would be.

Being able to choose something as best implies the use of a standard of value, a norm, to which possible choices are compared—in other words, a measurement system. We use many different measurement systems, but the one of interest here, the one that concerns how best to live, is part of a field called ethics. There are differing opinions as to what the word "ethics" should cover, but there is ancient precedent for saying that ethics is the subject of how we should lead our lives, and that is what will be meant here.

We have another word, "morality," that is closely related, and is taken by many people to be a synonym for ethics. Some, though, distinguish the two terms and there seems to be good reason to use ethics and morality with complementary rather than synonymous meanings.

Despite Henry's concern with ethics—that is, with finding the best way to lead his life—most people would say that morality was not applicable to him, because it applies only to the choices we make that will have impact on other people. A man alone on an island is not interacting with other people, and a hasty glance at a list of our common moral duties tends to confirm that they are not relevant to Henry's problems. Examples of morality are the duty to tell the truth to others, to avoid hurting others, and to help others in an emergency—all of which are types of social interaction.

The moral duties, however, seem to cover only part of the social choices we make. For instance, the choice of facial expression and tone of voice when greeting a customer who has interrupted our lunch is probably not a moral choice.

We also make many other choices beyond those that are primarily for the welfare of others. For example, there is the choice of whether to break into a run when we see the bus approaching the corner, the choice of which buttons to push to get what we want from an unfriendly computer, the choice of how much salt to put into the stew.

Choices of either type, social or not, to which morality is not applicable are called practical choices. Overall, the majority of our choices appear to be the practical choices and, in total, they probably affect our lives and those of others at least as much as the moral choices. Actually, every one of our choices probably affects the quality of life in some way and to some degree.

Since moral and practical choices can be correct or mistaken, we use measurement systems as the basis for judging the correctness of both. But the standards are different and, beyond that, the measurement systems used for moral and practical choices also differ considerably in the way they work.

Practical choices are made on the basis of the expected consequences of the actions. This places an important limitation on the degree to which we can be confident, at the time, that we are making the best choice. We usually have reason to believe the choice we are making is a good one, but we cannot tell how good until the action is over and the results are in. In fact, we may never be sure what the best choice would have been because we don't really know what would have happened had we taken a different action. In addition, we cannot be sure we are aware of all the actions that could have been taken.

In using this measurement system we compare the results to the standard—usually the goal we hoped to attain by the action. Most of our practical choices are aimed at specific objectives that are easy to adopt as standards.

The standards against which moral choices are judged are quite different. They are a set of moral duties that have been selected fundamentally on the basis of ethical intuition. The way the morality system functions, we can be sure that if we act in accordance with the proper moral duties, and do so with the proper motivation, we are taking the right action. We do not have to wait to see the results. The consequences of actions taken in accordance with duty are not morally relevant. An action is not judged to be wrong just because it does not work out well, any more than good consequences excuse a choice that is contrary to duty.

In addition to the differences in the way these two systems function, there is a large difference in the way they affect us emotionally. The person who makes poor practical choices is regarded perhaps as being foolish or misguided, but certainly not despicable, as we would regard the person who makes wrong moral choices.

The hold that the system of morality has on our attitudes is very strong. An activity that we engage in every day, namely, judging the actions of others to be moral or immoral, is a feature of the morality system. In contrast, the system used for practical choices deals in shades of gray, better or worse, being well- or ill-advised. In moral judgments, the motives of the actor are very important. In practical judgments, what the actor does is the focal point; motives are not particularly important. Emotions such as guilt, indignation, and abhorrence are aroused by moral transgressions, but not generally by practical actions, although the practical actions may have equally bad or good consequences.

Many of our most cherished ideals, such as natural rights, are outgrowths of morality. The duties of the morality system are really injunctions and are reminiscent of those we use to control children who are too small to understand why they should or should not do something. Perhaps these childhood injunctions prepare a mental niche in the child into which the moral duties later fit.

THE CONSEQUENTIALIST SCHEME

The purpose of this book is to present a theory that people in a sovereign state could use in developing an optimum set of societal rules. The theory is thus political in nature. But "optimum" means that the rules should be best for the people, so the political theory must be used in conjunction with an ethical scheme.

The political theory will work in conjunction with any of a variety of ethical schemes, but it covers a wide variety of situations that incorporate both moral and practical issues. It is helpful to use an ethical scheme that has the same broad range of applicability. Ethics provides principles for leading the best life, and all choices, both moral and practical, potentially affect the attainment of that best life. Thus we look for an ethical system that covers all choices, both moral and practical.

The expansion of morality to cover the whole range of choices does not appear feasible. Ethical intuition expands slowly at best and is unsuited to a wide range of practical issues, particularly when the latter change frequently. For example, we seem to have great trouble broadening morality to cover abortions, use of fetal tissues, animal experimentation, protecting our privacy from computers, and the many other changes stemming from the impact of technological progress on the sources of ethical intuition. On the other hand, the expansion of the decision apparatus used for practical choices into the area presently covered by moral principles has already been demonstrated by utilitarianism.

Utilitarianism traditionally uses pleasure or the absence of pain as the basis for the standard of value and assumes that pleasure can be measured, or at least estimated quantitatively. Choices are compared on the basis of how much pleasure they will produce in the whole population. In fact, the discussions of utilitarian theory often seem to be particularly concerned with the kinds of choices involved in morality. Such a focus carries with it a tacit acceptance of the distinction between moral and practical choices and leaves the impression of a reluctance to push the system back into the area of self-serving nonmoral choices. It also emphasizes choices by individuals for the good of society rather than choices for their own good or choices by society for the good of society. Because of these characteristics, as well as the use of pleasure as the standard, utilitarianism is not itself a desirable ethical system for use with the political theory.

However, the approaches to evaluation used in utilitarianism and in practical choices are similar; both are types of consequentialism. To satisfy the needs of the political theory, the ethical scheme to be used here is consequentialist and applied to the whole range of choices, from those by a person for his or her own ends to those by a society for the good of all.

The use of this approach to ethics is missing the familiar structure of moral duties and may leave the reader feeling unsatisfied. Nevertheless, many of the fundamental principles are the same as the duties of morality, although they are based on consequences rather than ethical intuition. They can, if one likes, be expressed as duties, although duty does not carry the same underlying meaning it does in a morality system.

STANDARD OF VALUE

The foundation of a consequentialist ethical system has to be a standard of value since all the ethical principles stem from that. Let us start with the premise that every action we initiate has a purpose. That is to say, it is done to bring about a particular future state of affairs. The phone rings; the receiver is picked up and carried to one's ear. This may well have been prompted by habit, but it is a purposeful action and the purpose is evidently to answer before the caller hangs up. This immediate purpose was, at some point, chosen because the person receiving the call wanted to find out who the callers were and what they had to say. This is a longer-range purpose. It is, in turn, intended to support a purpose of keeping in contact with people who have some reason to call.

There is a pattern here. Each action we initiate has an immediate purpose, which has been chosen to satisfy a longer-range purpose, which was chosen to satisfy a still longer-range purpose. This is not to say that we run through a lengthy list of interconnected purposes each time we make a decision. Many of the longer-range purposes have been reduced to habits, attitudes, practices, conclusions, and the like. However, it is evident that we have, within us, a hierarchy of purposes in which those of each layer are chosen to satisfy purposes in the next higher layer. As we progress up the hierarchy, the purposes become not only longer-range, but more general and abstract, and will probably stem from purposes chosen at progressively earlier times in our lives.

Essential to the operation of such a hierarchy must be some final overall purpose that can be used to resolve all conflicts between the layers of shorter-range purposes. This is equivalent to saying that each person has a general overarching purpose in life, probably something we are not conscious of on an everyday basis.

The functioning of a hierarchy of purposes does not provide a mechanism for choosing the overall purpose. That has to be something inherent, integral to the individual.

It would be helpful if we could test this idea by tracing the hierarchy back introspectively to find the overall purpose. Actually, this exercise leads to purposes that are so broad and vague that they do not satisfy the desire for a recognizable concept. Possibly practice would improve our ability to introspect. However, it seems likely that purposes at the upper end of the the hierarchy may not be available to our consciousness or may not be in the form of concepts. Perhaps these purposes reveal themselves as feelings, emotions, preferences, or the like. Perhaps they are the residue of decisions made early in life that are no longer remembered and may have occurred before we could talk.

The idea that we have a highest value, a self, a soul (in the nonreligious sense of that term) is something that most of us encounter from time to time. For example, there is the idea that a good painting reflects the most deeply held values of the artist and perhaps of viewers who feel particularly moved by it. Various psychological theories claim that mentally healthy people live in accordance with their essence. There is also the idea with which many people seem comfortable, namely, that they personally have a soul even though they are not religious. These ideas could well be ways of talking about the overall purpose or something close to it.

Ultimate purpose is the name that will be used in the discussion to designate this overall purpose, against which all the rest of our purposes are judged. Ultimate purpose is unique to each individual, but, like a fingerprint, may be very similar from one person to another. My suggestion, based on considerations outside the scope of this discussion, is that our ultimate purpose is to project our individual natures into the future by (1) extending our lives, (2) reproducing biologically, and (3) taking other actions that express our natures in some form that persists. Examples of this last category may be found in a wide variety of activities such as art, teaching, the construction of buildings or of human organizations, and so forth.

THE GOOD

Every action we initiate is purposeful and is done in order to bring about a goal that is some future state of affairs. The achievement of that goal is *the good* and thus the standard against which the choices we make and the consequences of our actions can he measured.

Nevertheless it is easy to find cases in which we succeed in achieving an immediate goal only to find that we do not progress toward the longer-term goal under which it is subsumed. We didn't telephone ahead, but raced through traffic to reach a store before it closed, only to find that it had not opened because of a holiday. In this case we made a mistake in choosing an immediate goal that was not the good.

Defining good in terms of most goals runs the risk that the goal was mistakenly chosen. The exception is ultimate purpose. Thus, ultimate purpose is the basic standard of the good and the proper standard for the present consequentialist scheme of ethics. Since each of us has his or her own ultimate purpose, this leads to the further conclusion that each has a personal standard of good and thus a personal standard for a consequentialist ethical scheme. This standard of good serves each of us as the basis for making the best choices.

While the discussion will continue on the basis of this consequentialist ethic, one should not forget that the political theory does not require that we accept consequentialism, or if we do, we need not accept the existence of ultimate purpose as defining the good. The political theory merely requires that we have some way of evaluating what is good for a person.

PERSONAL ETHICS AND SOCIETAL ETHICS

Henry's optimum choices, the choices that would enable him to make the greatest progress toward his ultimate purpose or enable him to lead the best life he could, depend on (1) his environment, (2) his capabilities, and (3) his ultimate purpose. None of these would be exactly the same for any other individual, so his optimum choices would be unique as well.

No doubt there were some broad principles that would have been of help to Henry. For example, the virtues of courage, persistence, carefulness, hard work, decisiveness, and the like would probably have been worth his time to cultivate. While Henry's optimum choices would have differed from the next person's, the applicable ethical principles would probably have been similar.

The consequentialist ethical system that uses an individual's ultimate purpose as the standard of good is here called *personal ethics*. Putting it another way, personal ethics is the class of the sets of consequentialist ethical principles that are applicable to individuals.

When other sailors settled on the island, the virtues appropriate in Henry's personal ethics would have expanded to include honesty, courtesy, friendliness, and so forth. Personal ethics is not limited to actions that directly benefit the actor and may advise doing things that are for the benefit of others. There is no suggestion intended here that personal ethics should emphasize short-range results such as pleasure. On the contrary, since ultimate purpose is a long-range standard, the purview of personal ethics can well extend beyond the lifetime of the subject. In fact we would expect personal ethics to recommend acting consistently in a way that is acceptable to the people around us who influence our environment.

Some of the common ethical concepts such as justice, rights, and responsibilities have not come up in the discussion so far. These are important ideas and must be accounted for in any ethical system, but they apply in situations where human beings live in a society. The word "society" will be defined in chapter 6, but it is enough here to say that Henry and the other men, living apart in the early days of the settlement on Comet Island, did not constitute a society. True, the men occasionally created social structures, as they did when they built the bridge or played chess, but these were quite temporary.

Obviously the men were headed toward the creation of a society, and when this occurred, these latter ethical concepts applied to them and to the society. The principles that incorporate these latter concepts will be here called the principles of *societal ethics*.

The important point to note at this stage of the discussion is that societal ethics does not use the same standard of value as personal ethics. In place of an individual person's standard of good, societal ethics must be based on a standard that reflects the interests of the whole group of individuals that compose the society.

Where two systems of ethics are based on two different standards of good, they will be independent of each other except insofar as the two standards are related. In general, the possibility of conflict between the two systems of ethics will exist. The theory developed here accepts the notion that both personal ethics and societal ethics will be in use concurrently in the same society, the former applicable to one realm, the latter to another.

As will be discussed later, societal ethics gives advice on the rules that should be adopted by the society, not directly on the actions to be taken. Personal ethics advises on the actions to be taken by individuals. Thus the two systems of ethics are not directly in conflict, although they may favor different choices in particular cases.

3

A Utopia

Three weeks after Henry arrived on Comet Island another ship, this time from the north, came sailing along, headed for the Tidy Isles. It was a sloppy ship with a lazy crew and a devious captain. The sailors moved listlessly about their duties. In contrast, the passengers—men, women, and children, all members of the New Socratic Society—sat in groups on the deck, disciplined, courteous, and solemn. Standing before them was Andrew, their leader. A large man with a ruddy face, white hair, and a long white beard, he wore a dark woolen mantle that extended to his ankles and flapped gently against his legs as the ship moved along.

"Beloved comrades," said Andrew, speaking loudly into the wind, "soon we will finish our cruise. We will disembark and start our life of the future. The captain tells me that the bountiful Ajax Island is close at hand and my own celestial observations confirm this. We expect to reach the island tomorrow and we must all prepare ourselves mentally for the next phase of our journey. Upon landing, you will be thrown into a struggle with manifold problems. You will be caught up in urgent quandaries and irritating difficulties. Your days will be filled with pressing tasks that will leave you neither time nor strength for the contemplation of life's important matters.

"In due course, these vexations will pass. But, before we enter this period of travail on the morrow and emerge again in a few months, triumphant and united in spirit, it is fitting that we spend our penultimate day aboard the ship immersed in the glories of philosophy." He paused, beamed at the members, and then waved his hand. "Each discussion leader will commence the reading and everyone will please join in the arguments with vigor."

The society members smiled back at Andrew as each group fell happily to reading aloud from traditional philosophy classics, arguing every point. Most of the sailors ignored this familiar rite. But one or two listened momentarily, then shook their heads in dismay and turned back to their appointed tasks.

The discussions continued all through the morning. Participants seized on the ideas, debating heatedly, oblivious to everything going on around them. At eleven, one man or woman from each group made his or her way below deck to relieve those who were guarding the society's key possessions. Then at midday the ship's bell rang for lunch. A member of each group rose, walked to the galley, brought back a tray of food, and set it on the deck in the center of the group. The ship's food was not very appetizing, but everyone reached over to the tray, took a portion and ate dutifully while the discussion continued unabated.

At mid-afternoon the discussions were still going strong and, although some were tired, each member kept on diligently trying to contribute ideas and reasoned reactions. In the group led by Andrew, one of the men begged leave to pose a question that was off the current subject. "Counselor Andrew, is it your view that good basically means good for a particular person?"

"Absolutely," said Andrew. "We must start with the fact that each of us, as Aristotle indicated, has deeply buried within him something fundamental in the nature of a goal or purpose, something of which we may be only remotely aware in our normal thinking. The measure of good, of what action is the best, is the degree to which the action brings a specific person closer to his fundamental goal. The same action may carry another person away from his fundamental goal and thus a particular action may be good for one person and bad for another.

"The New Socratic Society has to be concerned with this because your fundamental goals are the basis of the society's plans and decisions for you. But your fundamental goal is not something that you personally should worry about on a day-to-day basis. In my interviews with you on behalf of the society, I try to learn as much as I can about your personal fundamental goal and if I have done my job adequately, I know more about your goal than you do. In other words, your fundamental goal is something that you should know exists, but, as a member of the society, you ordinarily need not know much about it."

The group was silent. Then a red-headed woman spoke up. "Counselor Andrew, would it not then be your view that there should be a personal ethical system based on one's individual personal goal as the standard?"

Andrew waved his hand and a smile came over his face. "Absolutely, Alicia. Since identifying the good, which depends in turn on identifying a person's fundamental goal, provides the standard for ethics, we must conclude that we should be looking for an ethical system for each individual person based on what is the good for that person."

Alicia looked perplexed. "I know I've asked this before, but I'm afraid I still have difficulty reconciling your view that there are individual personal ethical systems, with the underlying organization of the New Socratic Society. Having personal goals and a personal ethical system doesn't seem to be consistent with the ideas that you have been teaching us and the types of behavior that you have been instilling in us."

Andrew shook his head. "It's perfectly consistent. But that's another subject, and it's getting late. The other groups are already headed for their chores. We must go along."

Alicia interrupted, holding up her hand. "Wait! Please, Counselor. The kind of ethical system that comes out of defining good in terms of what is good for each individual person has to lead people to being selfish. And yet you teach us that we should never do things on the basis of personal motives, which I understand to include all selfish motives and most of those that are unselfish."

Andrew was rising and the rest of the group followed his lead, but he smiled at Alicia. "It's not a short subject and we'll have to take it up at a later time." He put a hand on her shoulder. "Let me leave the subject by saying that the perfect way to reach your fundamental personal goal is through perfect obedience to a perfect plan for achieving the fundamental society goal."

The next day, the ship reached Ajax Island and anchored off a beach on the western side. The apathetic sailors prepared to ferry the passengers and luggage ashore in the ship's boats. Members of the society, baggage in hand, lined up on the deck in boat-sized groups, waiting for the transfer. One of the members, acting as operations supervisor, assigned groups to the boats in accordance with a copy of the unloading plan. The boats carried them, group by group, to the land, and they disembarked on the beach. By mid-afternoon nearly all the members were ashore with the society luggage, tools, weapons, agricultural supplies and animals, food and machinery, books, and nearly everything else the society had brought.

As they reached the shore, the passengers started to work. A supervisor, looking up from the first-day work plan, checked each member off, assigned the person to work in a party, and passed the individual on to a foreman. The society speedily constructed a temporary camp behind the beach, raising tents, digging trenches for sanitary purposes, establishing a ditch-wall around the camp for defense, and building facilities for cooking. Even the children were doing a share of the work, mostly by bringing in firewood.

The construction foremen were not the same as the discussion leaders, nor were they the supervisors who had managed the transfer from ship to shore. It was common in the New Socratic Society to shuffle job assignments and the composition of the work groups. The society considered it good for members to have some variety in their work. When the group was in a new environment and handling a new set of tasks, the society did more rotating of members to find those who had the most interest and ability at the various new jobs and to give them training.

It was late in the afternoon and it had been quite a while since the last boat from the ship had arrived on the beach. Suddenly a pause swept over the groups working in the camp. People stopped what they were doing, looked out at the ship and listened. They saw Andrew and his comrades standing at the rail facing the crew. Very faintly they heard the sound of angry voices.

A long moment passed. Then a shot was heard. Then three more shots. The crew appeared to fall back in confusion. People at the camp could see Andrew and his supporters spreading out along the side of the ship as though they had rehearsed the movements. The men from their society lowered three of the boats, swarmed down into one of them and rowed furiously toward shore towing the other two boats behind.

The crew reappeared on the deck of the ship, running for the two guns that the ship carried, one fore, the other aft. Others, armed with muskets, climbed up into the rigging. There were scattered shots from the ship, and angry shouts, but the boats were out of musket range and well on their way to shore. Some of the men on shore fired back at the ship to show they were armed.

Andrew and the men pulled the boats up onto the sand and motioned for everyone to take cover back in the dunes. "They butchered one cow and two of the pigs," panted Andrew. "On top of that, the lists showed they took some other supplies. We asked for payment. They refused. We'd already paid our passage so we took three of their boats in settlement."

"What about the guns?" asked one of the watchers.

"We spiked those, and took their powder when we saw the trouble coming up," said a man who had come in the boats with Andrew. "The sailors didn't understand what we were up to and didn't know we had the pistols until it got nasty."

"Weren't you afraid they would get their own pistols?" asked Alicia, rising a little from her crouched position behind one of the smaller dunes.

Andrew stood up. "I think they've decided to leave." He pointed to the ship, which was swinging around. "To answer your question, we chased them down below deck and shot into the doors and hatches to warn them not to come out. I'm sure they were arming themselves. The key was to be quick, take what we were going to, and leave. We couldn't have held them off any longer."

The society members gathered in little groups and continued talking. In another half hour the ship had disappeared over the horizon. The men stacked their weapons and everyone went cheerfully back to work.

Each person had a specific, well-defined job to do at all times, as well as a back-up assignment. The latter usually consisted of helping somebody who worked more slowly. From time to time, each member checked with a foreman for the latest instructions and practically never was anyone standing around at a loss for what to do next.

That evening a watch was posted and everyone but the guards slept soundly after the strenuous day.

The next two days were spent in getting settled. On the fourth day, three parties carrying weapons marched out along the shore and through the jungle to explore and map the island. A fourth party accompanied them, offshore, rowing one of the ship's boats.

The rest of the members busied themselves improving the camp. They worked steadily, taking brief rest periods. Some of the elderly took naps. Most of the members were comfortable doing the jobs they had been assigned, but occasionally someone did run into a problem. When that happened one or more of the others pitched in to help. From time to time, one of the group led them in songs as they worked.

Ten days later, four weary but pleased parties returned from their journey. They had made a careful survey of the whole island and found no other people. They reported that it was a fertile land with deer and boars and an abundance of fish. There were plenty of trees to serve as building material and more than adequate potential farm land. They had found several substantial fresh-water streams and sites suitable for the village.

The society put on a special dinner to welcome the explorers back and then held a general meeting. A reporter from each group recounted their adventures and described what they had found. Questions were answered, comments were made. Then Andrew and a small group of managers retired to a tent to choose a location for the permanent settlement.

A few days after that, the temporary settlement exploded with activity as though it were a beehive and the flowers had just opened. Several work parties set out for the chosen site. Two other parties surveyed a road to the site and set to work on the places that needed construction. Another party found an appropriate streamside location at the edge of the woods and built a makeshift water-powered sawmill. In a few weeks, trees were being felled and lumber produced.

The plans for all these activities had been worked out in advance, starting years earlier and continuing even on shipboard during the voyage. It only remained to adapt the plans to the requirements of the terrain. By the time four months had passed, the society had moved into the new wooden buildings of the settlement.

The New Socratic Society buildings were few but large, so they could each accommodate many members. The society's routines incorporated little privacy and even less modesty. Although the idea of sexual promiscuity would have been shocking to the society, provision was made for properly committed and authorized couples to be alone at reasonable intervals. Children were raised communally with their natural parents involved to the extent considered desirable for the children.

The members slept in dormitories and ate in the dining hall. Food was prepared in a kitchen in large pots and baking ovens by a team of cooks. Most of the adults settled into these or other regular jobs. The managers were an exception; they were required to cycle at intervals through all of the jobs they managed.

More buildings were erected: workshops, storehouses, a library; fences were strung, crops were planted, an orchard was started. The main village square was paved with stones from the creek bed. Shelters were built for the fowl and other domestic animals, thereby reducing the number of members required to care for them.

The society members told each other and Andrew how pleased they were with their new home. They were gracious people, disciplined, and polite. In day-to-day actions there was little emotional strain and never any violence. Everyone behaved as befitted a responsible person; the community was harmonious and pleasant.

Thus, in a relatively brief period, the society had brought itself up to a comfortable standard of living. It then impatiently met to reestablish the program of philosophical reading and argumentation. The program was considered more urgent than work on additional facilities, although the latter went on at a reduced pace.

The buzzing of many voices could be heard a hundred yards from the dining hall. The society was gathered in its discussion groups, arguing philosophy again. In one group, Andrew looked at Alicia.

"It seems like an age since we last met on the ship. You posed an important question and I expect the group would still like to hear an answer."

Alicia nodded.

"As I remember," he continued, "we had established that each member inherently has his or her own measure of the good and that each thereby has a specific, appropriate system of ethics. You questioned how we could reconcile this with our teaching that each member should ignore his or her personal goals and be completely devoted to the welfare of this society as a whole?" Andrew looked around the group. "Have I got that right?"

There were murmurs of agreement. Alicia nodded again and added, "That's what I had in mind."

"Each of us," said Andrew, "could in theory seek to live his life alone and maximize his progress toward his own personal goal."

"But people don't live alone," said Alicia. "Practically everybody lives among other people."

Andrew nodded. "I agree with you. Nevertheless, in some societies, people live alone in the sense of acting for their own personal motives even when they are physically part of a crowd. Now, I grant you they may do things to benefit their family or friends or even somebody for whom they feel empathy. But this person takes the action that is personally judged to be the best thing to do according to his or her own standard." He looked around at the group.

"The New Socratic Society, as we have been saying, is founded on the idea that teamwork, in which everyone cooperates in an organized, goal-seeking way, is vastly more productive than individuals running around in a confused throng, each following his or her own plan, no matter how enlightened the person is as an individual planner. I am confident that as a society we can produce a much greater amount of benefit than the total all of us together could produce, each working on what he or she thinks best."

Andrew paused. The group looked patiently back at him. "We have all experienced, especially in the last four months, the effectiveness of well-managed groups in getting things done. Even more important, our society is in a position to distribute benefits in such proportions that they do the most good. So the existence of the society and the way it operates is justified by its effectiveness in conferring good on each of us."

Alicia raised her hand again. Andrew nodded. "Yes," she said, "but what I wanted to know was how you justified the requirement that we act unselfishly at all times although the ultimate goal is to provide benefits to ourselves anyway."

"All right," Andrew continued, "the effectiveness of teamwork in our society, as in teams everywhere, requires that everyone work at all times for the objectives of the team. This, in turn, requires that somebody be in a managerial position orchestrating a coordinated set of actions by the team members to give the best overall result. The individual member may be given only a limited objective which does not appear very important or beneficial to him, but if he deviates from it the whole plan may go awry.

"You can see that it would both slow things down and worse, mix things up, if each member stopped to think about every order received, to see whether it coincided with what he thought best. We should never even think about what we personally judge would be best to do. Everything we do is done as an agent for the whole society and we do only what will be of most benefit to the society. In nearly all cases, this means following orders.

"At the same time, society's only purpose is to benefit each of us. Society takes full responsibility for everyone's progress toward his or her personal goal. Therefore, each of us constantly receives orders to do things that will be personally beneficial, such as participating in this discussion. But members are not free to choose to come here merely because they think they will enjoy the conversation or that it will do them some good. Members are here because society has said to come on the basis of a decision, as unbiased and objective as the managers can make it, that this is an appropriate benefit and will do them good.

"That's the way the society fulfills its objective. If we do what we are supposed to do, actions that benefit others as well as actions that benefit ourselves, without ever thinking about whom they benefit, society will be able to produce and distribute benefits in a way that maximizes good for all of us. Each of us will get far more than he or she might in some other way of doing things. And that's the reason I stress the avoidance of personal motives. And that's the reason a person's individual ethical system tells that person to give instant obedience to authorized directions and always work for the best interest of the society as a whole."

Andrew beamed at the group, then pulled out his watch, looked at it, and stood up. "Alicia, would you please take over the group? I have an appointment to start a series of the evaluation interviews with your niece. You all can understand, from what I've been saying, how important it is to talk things out with children as they grow up so that the society has the best possible understanding of their fundamental goals in life. Without that, the society would know less about the kind of benefits to provide, and our whole carefully designed societal mechanism would be less effective."

4

The Status Society

The New Socratic Society was designed by Andrew to be a community that would bring out the best in human beings, one in which each member would lead a worthwhile life with a special emphasis on philosophical reading and discussion. His vision attracted people of an intellectual bent who wanted to devote their lives to the contemplation of such ideas.

Andrew had recruited well and in its first years on Ajax Island the society functioned largely as he had envisioned. Its members acted in a diligent, conscientious, and cooperative way; performed their chores; worked together amiably, without being affected by questions about benefits and for whom they were intended, or whether the managers' directions were well-advised. They relished their participation in the philosophical discussions and were stimulated by Andrew and the intellectual climate. They felt that the society was efficient, effective, and just.

THE RULES OF THE NEW SOCRATIC SOCIETY

The change from each member's previous style of life was substantial, perhaps comparable to that of joining a monastery. Indeed, the society had many desirable monastic features: the pace of life was measured; everyone had an assigned job and daily routine, there was no competition, no need to worry, and very little uncertainty about any matter of significance. For most members the society was better than a monastery. They were unencumbered by religious requirements and came closer than monks to leading a biologically normal life with spouse and children.

While they neither signed a contract nor exchanged promises, the members understood that they could only be part of the society as long as they acted in accordance with its discipline and objectives. Andrew pointed out that in this society, the more control over their own individual actions that members were willing to give up, the more good they would all achieve. Since he was determined that the society lead its members to achieve maximum good, Andrew insisted that the society have full power over their actions. Specifically, he pointed out that the members as they participated in the society would make no choices for themselves except as the society directed them to, as part of their duties for the benefit of the society as a whole.

This may sound like an extraordinary sacrifice and, in fact, it sounded too intrusive to many prospective members. Andrew would not compromise on this principle and most prospects who were concerned about it declined to join. As a result the society did not contain conservative or middle-of-the-road people, but rather was composed of members who were prepared to make a strong commitment to the society's goal. The members relied on Andrew's promise that, in exchange for giving up acting on personal motives, they would receive their rightful share of the benefits generated by a whole society organized for the sole purpose of advancing their welfare.

Since the society assumed complete responsibility for the lives of its members, it had to provide benefits to them and orders for them for every minute of the day and night. This task required an extensive set of rules, developed by Andrew and the other managers, telling everyone what to do at all times. The rules were not onerous, but they were certainly complete and consistent. If members ate, it was because the society had decided they should eat. If members slept, it was because the society told them to sleep. The society always had a reason. Maybe it told them to sleep because it was providing them with a benefit or maybe because sleep would make them better workers, or more likely both.

This may sound as though it would lead to an impractical set of complicated minute-by-minute rules. Instead, the society sacrificed a certain amount of precision to make the overall program function smoothly. While in theory one member might need somewhat more or less sleep than the next, actually a bell was rung in the evening when it was time for everyone to go to bed and again in the morning when it was time to get up.

The word "rule" is used here in a broad sense to include any societal obligation for a member to act or refrain from acting. A rule can be written, oral, or merely understood, as in the case of a custom that has the force of a rule. The rules on Ajax Island included not only the equivalent of laws and ordinances, but also all the directions and orders given by the managers and foremen to get things done. Such directions and orders were usually oral, although occasionally they were in writing.

The rules in this society were *positive rules* that required action by the members, and were usually in the form "Do this." All the members' time, twenty-four hours a day, was accounted for by these positive rules, Thus, there was no need to have negative rules, ones that told the members what not to do; following the rules left members no room for deviating from the program or initiating actions on their own.

Despite these rules, the society was concerned that members might covet or even handle things that had not been assigned to them. Andrew made this sort of deviant behavior less likely by excluding decorative things, handicrafts, jewelry, and the like from the society. In addition, the lack of privacy minimized unauthorized actions because almost nothing could be kept secret.

Nevertheless, occasionally some members would take things that were not called for in their orders and not justified by being in the best interest of the society. This was not viewed as stealing, however. There could hardly be stealing in a society in which nobody owned anything. The society had no reason to formulate its position in terms of ownership rights. Rather, the deviant members were said to have behaved on the basis of personal motives. The society definitely took steps to prevent and penalize personal-motives behavior.

Personal-motives actions were deeds that actors performed on the basis of their own personal choices rather than as agents of the society. Personal-motives behavior included actions based on satisfying one's personal desires, longings, prejudices, views, likes, and dislikes or any factor other than what one was told to do or possibly some alternative action that was clearly better for society. It was assumed that no member would intentionally premeditate a personal-motives action, but the society recognized that all humans are fallible and that a propensity to indulge in personal-motives actions instead of obeying the rules is not an uncommon failing.

To keep personal-motives behavior from diverting members from their duties, Andrew asked everyone to keep an eye on fellow members. Anyone noting an example of personal-motives behavior was obligated to report it to the managers and they were instructed to institute a helpful group discussion with the transgressor immediately. If this was not enough, the society had rules that helped potential backsliders to act in accordance with their duties by threatening punishment if need be.

There was one case in which a member repeatedly behaved in a selfish way and the society concluded that he could not achieve the level of discipline required for membership. The society reluctantly expelled him, buying his passage to the mainland on a ship. The former member was provided, as he left, with clothing and a modest amount of money. There were also two cases in which members, on their own, decided they wanted to withdraw from the society. They were given the same exit benefits.

There were no serious crimes in the early years on Ajax Island. Everybody's time was fully occupied; nobody had unstructured leisure in which to brood or become disaffected, let alone get into mischief. Of course, the society had its share of people who developed mental disabilities. But everyone lived close together, the managers monitored the members closely, behavior alterations were quickly noticed and adjustments were made for or by the individual.

THE ROLE OF THE MANAGERS

The nature of the society put a considerable responsibility on the members who acted as managers. They had to make a vast number of rules, ranging from major policies to detailed directions for specific tasks. Apart from Andrew, their leader, the managers were divided into two groups, those who handled production and those who handled distribution.

The production managers worked out programs to generate benefits based on schedules of the desired benefits furnished to them by the distribution managers. In doing this, the production managers used a human-resources schedule, also generated by the distribution managers, listing the hours of the day each individual member would be available for production work. The production managers tried to use members' time efficiently, preferably at each person's highest skill. Because an individual's skills often did not match the production requirements, the actual usage to which people were put was not close to the ideal. The production managers, of course, had no pool of people from which to hire or to which to lay off as do businesses in most of the Western world. Rather, the managers' problems resembled more closely those of managers in an army.

The biggest problem for the production managers was motivation. It is natural for individuals to work for their own benefit, or for other personal motives. Inducing the same individuals to work as avidly for the benefit of the society required teaching them the proper attitude. The most important factor in teaching and maintaining highly motivated attitudes in the workers was consistency in the behavior and the attitudes of the managers.

As long as the managers' actions were obviously directed only to benefit the society, which was largely the case in Andrew's time, their subordinates noted this and conformed. As long as the managers worked hard at their jobs, it was not difficult to get the subordinates to work hard at theirs. On the other hand, if the managers pampered themselves in some way that was inconsistent with the needs of the society, they did substantial damage to the motivational fabric of the whole team. Managers who made arbitrary decisions, used their authority to play politics, or gave orders that were not directed to the best interests of the society, caused a reduction of societal efficiency by much more than the direct effect of their decisions.

Consequently, Andrew made sure that the managers were trained to be consistent in their actions, and to always make choices in accordance with the principles of the society. In general, he considered decisions that were consistently in accordance with the plans and best interests of the society more important than decisions that might be better solutions to near-term problems.

The managers supported this pattern of behavior by frequent discussion and criticism among themselves and by periodically subjecting themselves to criticism from the members in general meetings. Occasionally a manager, with the best of intentions, made a decision that might be viewed as deviating from these high standards. Managers were trained to immediately explain the basis for such an action to their subordinates and any others involved so that the action would not inadvertently cause damage to morale and motivation.

The management of benefit distributions was a more complicated field. The distribution managers not only allocated the benefits to the individual members but also monitored the members' responses to see how much good they received from the benefits.

Members were fed, clothed, housed, and their medical needs satisfied. Beyond that the principal benefit they received was participation in the philosophical discussions. As far as additional material benefits were concerned, Andrew did not believe they would be of much value to his members and so he discouraged suggestions that the society develop more of the land, invest in capital equipment, or accumulate consumer goods other than philosophy books.

Of course, the members did have secondary, though often pressing, needs ranging from art to athletics and socializing to sex. Andrew did not see much good to be gained by any significant commitment to these activities either, but as the society worked out its rules he accommodated the views of others and had the managers incorporate some of each of these activities into the program. Andrew's fundamental position was that members should sublimate their drives into their participation in the philosophical discussions, and he asked that the managers help the members learn to do this.

In the early years of the society, the managers were ever mindful that their authority over the members arose from their responsibility for the members' entire welfare. They were very conscious of being authorized to use this authority for no other purpose, certainly not for themselves.

THE STANDARD OF SOCIETAL ETHICS

Since ethics addresses the question of how best to live one's life, and since the society took the responsibility for ordering its members to live their lives in the way the society judged to be optimal, it was very important to Andrew that an appropriate set of ethical principles be developed and that the society be run in accordance thereto. Andrew drew a distinction between the combination of services and material things that were helpful to an individual and the results of the individual's use of these services and material things. The services and material things themselves he called *benefits*. The effect that occurred when a person utilized a benefit and was thereby helped toward his or her ultimate purpose Andrew called *good*. It should be noted that while Andrew used the term "fundamental goal," the equivalent term "ultimate purpose," introduced earlier, will be used in this discussion.

Andrew had engaged in an extensive period of meditation before selecting the system of ethics that would guide the society. He was familiar with a number of the systems that had been used in the past. The religious systems were not appropriate because his members were not believers. There were also systems of morality based on sets of duties and moral distinctions that were grounded on ethical intuitions. Since the members of his society came from a variety of European backgrounds, they agreed on many of these intuitive preferences, but not all of them. Andrew was wary of systems based on intuitions and could not honestly see how to defend any particular list of intuitive preferences with enough objective arguments to justify insisting on agreement from those who didn't already share the same intuitions.

Andrew sought a system of ethics that would lead him toward the welfare of all the members of the society, one in which the progress of each member was of equal concern, and one that would have the members enjoying greater progress toward their individual ultimate purposes than under any alternative standard. Thus, rather than an ethical system based on duties, he chose one based on a societal goal.

The standard he chose was the maximum total good for all of the society's members. Andrew concluded that good for each individual had to be judged in reference to that individual's ultimate purpose, even recognizing that individual ultimate purposes would be difficult to identify and the degree to which each was being approached would be difficult to quantify. He expected to learn more about how to do this as he went along.

Andrew pictured the members' purposeful behavior as though they were all climbing their own personal mountains. The members' ultimate purposes were to reach their respective summits, although this represented perfection and was hardly possible. Actions were judged as good to the extent that they resulted in the members' making progress up their respective mountains. The mountains varied in difficulty and the members in their ability to climb. Left to their own devices, members would try, as best they could, to climb as high as possible. According to Andrew's standard for societal ethics, the society should help them and endeavor to maximize the total gain in altitude made by all of its members, giving progress by each member the same weight.

Andrew considered several ways in which one could be said to maximize good according to this standard. One possibility would be to maximize the amount of good that could be provided if everyone were given the same amount and kind of benefits. This simple approach would have been acceptable to the society members, but it did not appeal to Andrew. He knew that giving the same benefits to different members would lead to differing amounts of good from member to member. He was convinced that the total amount of good for society would probably not be as high as in some other schemes. For example, feeding everyone the same foods would probably not maximize good if some of the members had food allergies, and feeding everyone the same amount wouldn't maximize good if the society was made up of people who varied in the amount of food they needed.

Another approach would have been to distribute the benefits to members in proportion to their contributions to the production of benefits. This would have the advantage of motivating the members to be more productive. However, since Andrew did not regard material benefits above a comfortable minimum as very important, he didn't think there would be any problem motivating the members to produce all they ought to have. The most important social benefit was participation in the philosophical discussions, and he shrank from the task of rating members on their respective contributions.

Andrew concluded that the proper way to maximize good was to map out individual detailed programs for members to make maximum progress toward their ultimate purposes, consistent with the benefits level that the society could maintain. This required the managers to make allocations among members, i.e., choices of whether to give a benefit to this member or that.

Andrew was familiar with the principle of diminishing utility, indicating that, after a specific amount of good had been reached, each increment of a given benefit for a given person produced less good. Thus, other things being equal, the first bite of dinner did the most good and the last bite the least. Assuming this was applicable to the allocation problems, the principle would tend to drive distribution in the direction of giving benefits first to those most in need. Diminishing returns was a major consideration in Andrew's calculations of maximizing good.

Of course consideration had to be given to other types of situations, too. Some individuals were physically or psychologically unable to use certain kinds of common benefits, so that more total good would be done by depriving them and conferring the benefits on others. Also there were threshold situations, such as learning the philosophy of some of the less articulate sages. In these cases, the first increments of benefit seemed to do little good, but there was considerable good done by later increments of the benefit after the person got the hang of it.

In order to lay a foundation for solving the distribution problems, Andrew interviewed each member at length to get an idea of each person's ultimate purpose. In addition, Andrew and his managers kept careful watch on each member's use of the benefits, matching that use against the person's ultimate purpose, to see how much good was derived.

SOCIETAL ETHICS APPLIES TO RULES

Morality imposes duties on people to satisfy obligations to others. Utilitarian systems ask that people do what is best for society. Andrew thought it was a mistake to require that the members as individuals solve the problems of society or even of other individuals. Individuals are frequently not in a position to know how to solve other people's problems.

This is not to suggest that Andrew was unsympathetic to the objective. In fact his whole society was organized to solve the broader social problems. But it used a planned, coordinated, team approach that identified, evaluated, and then acted to solve societal problems.

Andrew concluded that in contrast to personal-ethics principles, which clearly applied to a person's own choices and actions, the principles of societal ethics should apply to the choosing of rules by the society and not directly to the choosing of specific actions by individuals.

If an individual's action was seen to have been a mistake, but had been done in accordance with the rules of the society, then it was the rules that were wrong and should be changed. If an unfortunate action reflected someone's acting deliberately contrary to the rules, then the rules for handling such a person and his or her behavior might be the thing that needed to be changed. If the rules were not the problem, then it must be in the nature of the offender, or something else that was not part of ethics.

Parenthetically, Andrew would probably have come to the same conclusion if he had been looking at a society in which the rule broken was a negative rule. In any society, people who deliberately break rules reflect either inadequate rules or something about the individual's personal ethics. In the latter case, it is not a matter of societal ethics, since societal ethical principles apply to the choice of rules and not to individual actions.

There are two bases for an individual's actions: (1) preferences and (2) obligations. There are also two ethical systems involved, personal ethics and societal ethics.

For people living in the society, Andrew tried to avoid conflicts between the advice provided by the two ethical systems; he simply eliminated personal ethics from the decision-making process. In order to do this, he eliminated personal preferences and individually arranged personal obligations as a permitted basis for actions. A society that uses only negative rules operates on the opposite basis, excluding societal obligations as the basis for (positive) actions.

In Andrew's society, the members were precluded, by every means the society could reasonably muster, from choosing actions on the basis of their personal motives. Personal preferences were directly excluded, and the individual was given no opportunity to initiate personal obligations. The members of the New Socratic Society were required to make all their choices and take all their actions on the basis of societal rules based on societal ethical principles.

THE STATUS SOCIETY

Andrew never tired of comparing the internal operation of his society to the operation of a team competing in a sport. One of the characteristics of a team, particularly visible in sports, is that its members have varied roles because a team functions by coordinating different activities thus making direct use of division of labor. In turn, this requires the existence of differences in the relationships between the team and particular team members, relationships expressed, for example, in the specific rules that reflect the different tasks that the team wants its members to perform. Thus, on a football team, the middle linebacker has a different set of instructions, makes a different contribution, and thus has a different relationship with the team than does the left guard. In addition, a team often treats members differently in the distribution of pay, perquisites, and so forth.

These different relationships can be summed up in the word "status," which is often used with an adjective primarily to convey a connotation of high or low position. It will be used here in a more basic sense, without such a connotation. The *status* of a member of a society means here the specific relationship between the society and the individual member, as reflected in the rules that apply to that member. "Middle linebacker" and "left guard" are words that signify statuses on a football team. "Discussion leader" and "cook" were terms that signified statuses in the society.

The New Socratic Society definitely functioned as a team. A team requires status distinctions between its members in order to get the full benefits of teamwork. The group would not be functioning as a team if all the members had the same specific instructions. Teams are positive-rule societies, and all positive-rule societies from monasteries on have these status distinctions. Societies of the positive-rule/team kind will thus be referred to as *status societies.*

As a practical matter, in status societies of more than a few members there is also usually a grouping into classes of members who have the same or similar status. Each of the eleven football players on the field has a distinctly different role and thus a different status. On the football squad, however, it is necessary to have several individuals who are substitutes for each of those on the field. For example, there may be three or four of the middle linebackers and as many of the left guards. Thus these terms are also the names of classes of players who have the same status because they play the same role. Being on the second team is another indication of the player's status and his membership in a different class. The New Socratic Society had many such classes and each member belonged to several.

ETHICAL PRINCIPLES

The principles applicable to the choosing of rules in a status society are its ethical principles. Many of the rules in such a society can be very detailed: for example, the directions by the chef to the cooks. The principles applicable to this kind of detailed rule—such as cooking vegetables only till crisp or cooking slowly with moisture meats that have substantial amounts of connective tissue—will not be discussed here. Such detailed rules where the consequences of actions can be quickly evaluated tend to evolve easily into desirable forms if the people involved are open-minded and perceptive.

Consider instead the ethical principles that apply to the longer-range rules. Some ethical principles, such as the need to act as the agent of society instead of acting on the basis of one's personal motives, apply generally to all parts of a status society. Other principles are applicable mainly to the production rules or to the distribution rules.

PRODUCTION RULES

The production rules are intended to result in the creation of appropriate benefits as efficiently as possible. The ethical principles guiding one to a set of rules that would accomplish this are probably similar to the principles appropriate for setting up and running production organizations in any society. They focus on increasing the productivity of the labor force, assuring the quality of the product, cutting down on waste, protecting the environment, minimizing capital requirements, and so forth. Among such principles are those about the proper emphasis to be given to various goals, about involving all the workers in the goals, about organizational structures, about the specific technologies involved—principles not typically labeled "ethics" in a morality system. A great many of these principles are known and taught in business and technical schools and on the job.

In dealing with positive rules, the most straightforward way to evaluate a proposed rule is to compare estimates of the societal productivity (or other societal characteristics of concern) with and without the rule. Incremental evaluation of a proposed rule, in which there is an attempt to trace and evaluate the consequences of the change, is useful diagnostically and requires much less effort but is theoretically less accurate. The effect of each positive rule depends on many other rules, just as the value of one player's directions on a football play depends on the directions to the other team members. A new instruction may point out a better route for the ball carrier to run, but the play will lose yardage if the instructions to the left guard are not changed so that he blocks a different tackler. New rules are often beneficial or detrimental because of many small shifts rather than one or two large, identifiable incremental factors.

On the other hand, projections of total good for a full society of even modest size, with and without a proposed rule, may take far too much effort to be practical for estimating the effect of a new rule unless a good mathematical model is available. Thus the managers may have little choice but to assess proposed rules by incremental approximations. Society has a hierarchy of goals, and may evaluate short-range rules by the standard of the short-range goals they are intended to reach. If the rule does not seem likely to affect other parts of the system, the incremental approximation may be good enough to serve as the basis of a decision. Most rules are justified this way. The city council passes a rule to create a subway so fewer riders will drive downtown and so the highways will be less crowded. Unfortunately, such predictions of incremental economic and sociological consequences are often unreliable.

A status society also normally has a hierarchical organizational structure built of *subsocieties,* for example, departments, divisions, sections, groups, etc. A subsociety is organizationally separate but integral to the parent society. The sawmill and the kitchen in the New Socratic Society are examples. Subsocieties share the long-term goal of the parent society, but have their own short-term goals as well. A proposed rule for a subsociety may often be adequately evaluated by estimating how much it contributes to accomplishing the subsociety's goals. For example, the kitchen could have evaluated the savings in labor and supplies by adding an oven, and this might have been enough to justify a decision to do that.

DISTRIBUTION RULES

Managing distribution is a much more complicated and demanding field than managing production, and the choices pertaining to it are more difficult. The ethical principles in this area reflect the goal of apportioning the benefits so that maximum total good is achieved.

The major underlying principle is that progress toward good for one member should be considered of the same importance as progress toward good for any other member. It does not follow, however, that a status society should attempt to achieve equal progress toward each individual's ultimate purpose. Many members can absorb benefits and show progress up to some point and then show very little further progress on receiving further benefits. This is not at variance with the situation on the production side. In a similar way, different members will be capable of different amounts of work. It can only be required that all contribute what they are capable of when fulfilling their assignments.

With proper management, the amount of work that society receives from each member and the amount of benefits it furnishes to him or her will vary, depending on what is optimum to produce the maximum total good. The managers in the New Socratic Society felt that to some degree the best contributors were also the ones who could make the best use of benefits, but the managers were careful not to let this perception affect their decisions, which were made on a case-by-case basis.

In a status society, the distribution of benefits corresponding to the basic needs of food, clothing, shelter, and medical assistance should be relatively simple, requiring mostly the matching of the needs of particular members—size of clothing, type and amount of food and medicine, and so forth. Moreover, it should be easy for the managers to see whether members use such basic-need items to achieve good for themselves. If the members don't eat the meals or wear the clothing, the manager knows that the society has a problem.

One of the most important ethical principles in a status society is that the management process, particularly in distributions, be guided by monitoring the effects and estimating the amount of good brought about. Without the monitoring, managers are not equipped to make their decisions on a sound basis.

While most people share the same basic needs, their goals beyond this in a normal population will cover a wide range and the managerial task of efficiently allocating benefits for such goals can be very complicated. The managers on Ajax Island benefited from the fact that Andrew had simplified the problem in much the way a monastery does, by selecting only members who have the same special overriding interest. Thus, the only major benefit Andrew expected the New Socratic Society to confer, beyond satisfying basic needs, was the philosophical discussion.

Even on Ajax Island it was not easy to balance the distribution so that everyone received a proper share. A distribution manager started with the estimate of how much good each benefit would do for each member. One complication was that the production jobs were good for some members and deleterious for others. It was not the production manager's job to adjust the program for these factors. Rather, the distribution managers had to account for them in their calculations.

The distribution managers assumed that an hour of the philosophical discussion produced the same amount of good in each member. Further, it was assumed that the second hour of discussion did incrementally less good for every member on the same schedule of diminishing utility, and so forth. This simplification permitted the distribution managers to balance things out in a way that seemed to be at least approximately valid. Given the differences in the members, their work requirements and benefit receipts sometimes developed odd patterns. Occasionally, for example, the calculations worked out in such a way that some individuals spent substantially more hours a week than the average member on the production side, particularly if they were exceptionally skilled at it and got some good out of it.

Another important ethical principle applicable to the status society generally is that, to the extent practical, the rules should incorporate the results of the value judgments involved, so that the member following the rule will only be judging facts. For example, if the logger foreman came across a tree of the type and size specified by the sawmill manager and the woodsman, he was supposed to cut it down and bring it to the mill. He was not asked to consider other aspects of the operation: the type of lumber needed by the builders, the place of the tree in the ecology of the forest, the aesthetic qualities of this kind of wood, etc. All these factors affected the value of felling the tree, but they were to be judged by others who, in turn, made their choices based on orders that required them to find facts, not make value judgments. Somewhere along the line values had to be judged, but the idea was to minimize and formalize these judgments.

It is very important in a status society that the ethical standard be kept constantly in mind. Otherwise, various personal motives will intrude and destroy the societal-ethics virtues of the system and its effectiveness for maximizing good.

5

A Social Contract

The widening reputation of Comet Island as a dumping ground for insubordinate sailors led to a slow but steady procession of maroonings. Some of the newcomers tried to find a way back to civilization, but no ship would have them. To be an inhabitant of Comet Island was to be a marked man.

Most of the inhabitants found life on the island not unpleasant. Their number was still low, relative to the size of the island. Each man created his own place to live, built his hut, planted his garden, developed facilities for storing food, and somehow took care of the rest of his needs. None of them was about to have somebody else tell him what to do. However, in spite of their feelings of independence, the sailors inevitably saw more of each other as their numbers increased. They did more trading and selling and developed more social contacts.

By and large, everyone got along amicably. But as the number of interpersonal contacts grew, the incidence of serious disagreements increased. There were disputes over boundaries, claims and counterclaims of ownership of animals killed in hunting, and complaints about people stealing from gardens. Henry began to worry about his own safety. What if somebody with bad intentions crept up on him in the night? He began to notice more things missing from his garden and suspected that the cause was more than just animals. His chores seemed harder; he enjoyed life less.

Neighbors visited him to complain and voice their concerns. They pressed him, as the original settler, to come up with a solution and exert some leadership. Finally, Henry concluded that the inhabitants of the

48

island were ready to agree on some basic rules. He suggested holding a meeting in a meadow in foothills near the center of the island. His friends applauded, got him to set a date, and passed the word around.

It was ten o'clock in the morning in the grassy, amphitheater-shaped meadow surrounded by jungle. All four dozen inhabitants of Comet Island were there. Half of them stood talking in groups. The rest were loners who sat apart on the grass, watching silently. Henry found an abandoned anthill about three feet tall, kicked it, and seeing no ants come out, kicked off more dirt until he had a platform about two feet high. He stepped up to stand on the top. Several of the men clapped their hands and whistled for silence.

"Thank you for coming," said Henry. "I called this meeting because a number of you have told me you think we ought to establish a society."

"Now wait a minute," said Jake, an old man wearing a dirty leather hat with unkempt pieces of hair sticking out from under the brim and a scraggly stubble on his chin. He peered up at Henry from his position in the front row. "I don't get along well in societies." Jake turned to glare back at some of the others who were muttering and giving him hard looks. Then he growled at Henry. "All right, all right, what you got in mind?"

Henry said, "I'm proposing that we agree on some basic rules, so that every man will know what's expected of him. We all enjoy our freedom and I have no intention of reducing its value, but if everyone acts as though he can do anything he wants, this place is going to be chaos."

"Hear! Hear!" said one of the men standing in the back, and half a dozen others echoed him.

Henry continued, "I don't personally have any specific complaints." He straightened up and nodded at the man in the back, "But, I hear it said that we have already started down the road to developing dangerous problems. Several of you have told me you are sure somebody will get killed in the next three months. With more new men coming onto the island, it's going to get worse and worse."

"Okay," said Jake, "we all understand that being free isn't the whole story and that it's the value of the freedom that counts."

"Exactly what I had in mind," interrupted Henry. "It's worth giving up some of our freedom, especially some of the parts we don't intend to use anyway, so that the part we do exercise is worth more. When I first lived on this island, I was free to go anywhere and do anything. But I spent most of my time in the area around my hut. And it wasn't nearly as interesting as it is now, even though there are many parts of the island where I can no longer do anything I please.

"I wasn't concerned when the first of you landed because you settled down in areas that weren't of much interest to me. But now, with so many people here, I'm beginning to worry about the value of my freedom to use the land I really want, the part around my hut. What I propose is that we divide up ownership of the land on a formal basis."

"Nobody's going to tell me what to do," said Jake stubbornly.

It was getting hot in the middle of the amphitheater and some of the men shifted over into patches of shade under the trees. Henry wiped the sweat from his forehead and said, "All right, the rules won't tell anybody what to do."

Jake said, "I'll bet."

Henry glared at Jake. "Shut up, Jake. The rules I'm going to propose are negative. They don't tell any of us what to do. They tell us what not to do. That may not mean much to you, but there's a big difference. You think about it, Jake, while we get on with the meeting."

"That sounds all right if all the rules apply exactly the same to all of us," said one of the men sitting a little way back.

Henry said, "Yes, that's part of the deal. It's one of the advantages of negative rules." Some of the men looked puzzled, but others were nodding their heads.

By noon many of the men were participating vigorously in the meeting and it sounded like the bargaining in a Middle Eastern market. Men shouted out proposals for rules they wanted, and others shouted back reactions for or against, depending on how they personally would be affected. Nearly always, someone objected to even the most obvious rule. Arguments started and often matters came to an impasse. Then someone would suggest a compromise, sometimes one in which the approval of a rule proposed by one set of people was traded for approval of a rule some other group wanted.

When the talk about rules began to quiet down, the subject was switched to land boundaries and this created an even bigger uproar. Many of the men were speaking at once and the clamor irritated the rest. Finally one of the loners disgustedly drew a fifty-foot-long map of the island in a dried-up mud puddle at the center of the meadow. Each man marked the boundaries he thought he was entitled to and the meeting settled down to a concurrent series of arguments between neighbors. Henry and some others were drafted to act as arbitrators and were able to get many of the neighbors to reach agreement.

However, other boundary disputes went on well into the evening, with men arguing by the light of bonfires. The men began to get tired and some of them became hoarse. Increasingly they were willing to give up small points to get things settled. By midnight, only a few pairs of holdouts were left adamantly maintaining their opposing positions. Irritated onlookers clustered around each pair and listened to the arguments. Impatiently, the listeners proposed arbitrary compromises, which were angrily rejected by both sides. The crowd of onlookers began shouting, threatening, even physically coercing in some cases. Eventually agreement, albeit reluctant in the minds of some, was reached in all cases.

The social contract and boundary descriptions with sketch maps had been written out as the discussions went along by three of the more educated men. The contract itself listed the rules. The boundary descriptions and maps defined both the private properties and areas to be owned in common. The scribes laid their papers out near the bonfires and the men gathered around reading and discussing them. Finally all of the inhabitants, many disgruntled, lined up and signed the contract and maps, muttering about the parts they didn't like.

The first rule was that everyone had to refrain from interfering with anyone else's private property. There were two pages spelling out what this meant. Private property included a man's person, his land, and his personal possessions. Some of what was meant by interference was defined and examples were listed.

The second rule defined common property and how it was to be used. Common property included the air, the ocean, a lake on the south end of the island, transportation corridors marked on the maps, most of the jungle, the mountain, and the beach below high tide. Common property was free for all to use. The basis for choosing things as common property was that they were so abundant, relative to the expected use, that all the inhabitants could use as much as they wanted.

Nonetheless, the rules did put limitations on the uses to which common property could be put. There was to be no waste or pollution, no use that would not be restored by nature in the normal course of events, no use for mining or even farming. There were traffic and priority rules so men using the same general pieces of common property at the same time would not interfere with each other.

After signing the agreement, most of the men got drunk and slept the last few hours of the night on the ground. The next morning they headed back to their homes quarreling and complaining all the way.

Adopting the rules had a pronounced effect. It markedly increased the level of activity on the island as the men worked to improve their properties. Fences and walls were put up to indicate boundaries and possession. Trees were felled, crops were planted, wild pigs were penned, buildings were built, and all manner of furniture and tools were fabricated. A substantial increase in trading developed. A market sprang up on Fridays at the social-contract meeting place. The men who had extra fruit or meat began to trade them to others. Quickly this kind of activity led to specialization. Men enlarged their orchards, planted more grain, began to make garments and shoes, or tried producing something else that they thought others would buy. Most of the men had had a little money with them when they were marooned and this circulated.

Those who settled on the island after the rules had been adopted were invited to sign the agreement and all of them did. Some purchased pieces of land if they had the money. Others got jobs working for somebody else. Many of the newcomers found it was better to work at a trade than farm. Landowners rented and sold small pieces of land for people to use for houses, workshops, and stores. Three villages sprang up, with craftsmen and merchants.

The merchants led the way in developing commercial relationships. They extended credit to customers and made contracts with craftsmen to produce things that the merchants felt they could sell. One of the newer settlers started a bank and issued money. Ships began to stop at the island for commercial purposes and after that, the trade with the outside world grew steadily.

The village on the harbor at the south end of the island grew particularly quickly. Two shipyards there competed to build ships for the fishermen who had settled on the island. Three years later, the shipyards began to build bigger ships to haul things back and forth from the mainland. A shoemaking factory was started, the first on the island to be owned by a company that issued shares. A packinghouse and leather tannery were also established, along with a large blacksmith shop that made useful things out of iron. Clustered around these larger businesses were small shops, leathergoods makers, gunsmiths, cobblers, and so forth.

Many of these activities came as an outgrowth of another important event that occurred six months after the rules on Comet Island had been established. A problem developed on Babo Island, the next island to the north, which was inhabited by a tribe of handsome brown-skinned Polynesians. They had arrived from islands far to the north and west a hundred years before Henry. The tribe lived in several villages, practiced an age-old culture, and had plenty to eat and drink.

The Babo Island population had been growing; there had been some encroachment on hunting and fishing grounds. A disagreement developed between the southernmost village and the others. Two men from northern villages were killed in the south of Babo under circumstances that their relatives found suspicious. The controversy grew until finally all the villages, except the southernmost, held a general meeting and decided to go to war. The tribe's sacred beverage was distributed to the gathering and a lengthy dance started. Under the hallucinogenic effect of the beverage, the Polynesians danced themselves into a state of righteous anger and disregard for personal safety. Finally, at dawn they burst forth from the gathering and streamed toward the southernmost village. Arriving, they found it abandoned.

The previous evening, the chieftain of that village, foreseeing the outcome of the meeting and knowing that his warriors would be greatly outnumbered, concluded that his people would be wiped out. He took immediate action. The villagers loaded everything they could into twenty-four canoes. Then, with all the men, women, and children aboard, the villagers paddled toward Comet Island.

The Polynesians knew Comet and Ajax islands well, but hadn't bothered to settle there because they were happier living together on one island. They knew that Ajax Island had been settled and that a few Europeans were now living on Comet Island. However, they thought there was still plenty of room on Comet Island and did not expect that its inhabitants would dare to oppose them.

The next morning the canoes landed on the north end of Comet Island. The weary villagers waded ashore, pulled the canoes up on the beach, unloaded their belongings, and began to settle down. As it happened, this piece of land belonged to Jake. He came running down to the beach protesting angrily at the top of his voice, waving his gun, ordering them to leave at once. They waved their spears at him. He backed off and fired a shot which wounded one of the warriors. Several others ran at him, throwing their spears, one of which grazed his arm. Jake backed off some more, reloaded, and shot again, killing one of the warriors. The villagers were momentarily thrown into confusion and Jake took the opportunity to run away as fast as he could.

Jake, having one of the few horses on the island, galloped off to see Henry, who was hoeing his garden. Jake jumped down, launching into bitter complaints about the invasion. He demanded that something be done.

"But Jake," said Henry, "you were one of the fellows who was so insistent that none of the rules tell you what to do."

"What's that got to do with it?" said Jake.

"It means that nobody can go around and tell anybody else that he is obliged to come down and fight off your invaders." Henry shook his head. "The only thing we can do is see how many want to volunteer." Jake looked at him in astonishment. Henry smiled sympathetically. "I've got some bandages in here. Why don't you sit down and let me fix up your cut? Then, while you rest up, I'll go out and see if I can find some volunteers."

The news spread rapidly, and in spite of Henry's skepticism, most of the men on the island joined the posse. The group that descended on the Polynesians two days later matched them in numbers of men and had firearms to boot. In the short battle that followed, several of the warriors were killed. The rest scrambled into the canoes and paddled furiously back to Babo Island.

The women and children, crouching among the palm trees and sand dunes during the fight, gradually came forth and looked at the victors. Jake gyrated around angrily, adamant that they could not stay on his land. The women started toward the remaining canoes gesturing an offer to launch them and follow the warriors.

Henry and the other men blocked them from the canoes and conferred. They recognized the opportunity to solve a problem that had bothered them, the absence of women. They decided it would be proper to divide up the women and children as a booty of war. The men circulated among the women and picked out mates for themselves. There were several fights among men who had chosen the same woman, but fortunately there were almost enough women to go around. The children went along with their mothers.

For several months thereafter, the men on Comet Island nervously expected another invasion by the Polynesians. They knew there were many more people on Babo Island than Comet Island; next time the warriors would be better organized. The Comet Islanders were pleased with the wives they had seized and the men were resolved to keep their new families. As time wore on, there was no invasion and no sign of hostile activity from Babo Island. Eventually the men learned that the warriors from the southernmost village returning to Babo Island had been seized and enslaved. The high chief and the chieftains of the other villages had no interest in recovering their families for them.

The women and children seemed to be content with their new husbands and fathers and all of them learned at least a smattering of English, the island language. Their presence resulted in the creation of a family atmosphere on Comet Island. To a substantial degree, it was in response to the needs of these new families that the production of goods increased, villages were built, farms improved, and all manner of new facilities constructed. A year after the invasion, teachers began to enroll some of the children in schools.

Nevertheless, there were new problems to face. The Polynesian women, no matter how well instructed, did not understand the finer points of the society rules and did not always observe European formalities. They didn't place the same emphasis on the literal keeping of promises and they didn't understand the mixed-up money system. The men had several fights that started because the women were susceptible to being duped by some of the less honorable men.

One day, Henry was talking to his friends about it. "You know we really ought to get the women to sign the social contract," he said. "The children, too, for that matter."

"But, Henry," said one of the others, "they don't understand the rules. Neither my wife nor any of the rest of them would understand what they're agreeing to. Each of us takes full responsibility for ourselves. If we make a promise, including the ones in the agreement, we keep it. If we make a bad deal, we swallow the loss and go on. The women and children brought up in that Polynesian tribe don't understand these ideas. They are used to being in a more paternalistic system where they have a chief to tell them what to do and make sure they get help."

"You've got a point," sighed Henry. The group sat for a moment mulling the problem. Finally Henry tried again. "I've got it. We have been assuming that every person on the island should be a member of the society, as long as he behaves himself. Suppose the family were the membership unit. One member of the family, the man, could represent the family and sign the contract on behalf of the family. Then it would be up to him to see that all the members of his family observed the rules. People couldn't take advantage of the family without involving the man, because promises by others in the family wouldn't count."

This idea was adopted and written into the agreement. Thereafter most of the society members were families. However, single men and single women who were judged to have integrity and the capability of taking responsibility for themselves were also permitted to sign the social contract and be members.

6

The Free Society

DEFINITIONS

Several of the words used in this book have been given restricted meanings. Several more are discussed below.

The human organization on Comet Island was described as a society after the social contract had been set in place, but not before. A *society* is defined here as having two constituent elements: (1) a set of rules, plus (2) a group of members who are obligated to follow that set of rules. The members of the society are usually individual human beings, but they may also be societies, such as families in the Comet Island society or sovereign states in the society of nations.

The basic societies on Ajax and Comet islands are of a type called here a *primary society,* one that imposes its rules on all people located within an area of the Earth's surface enclosed by its geographic boundaries. Within its territory, adherence to the rules of a primary society is compulsory, insofar as the society can, or wishes to, enforce them. Primary societies are the sovereign states of the world. One could argue that the society on Comet Island was not a primary society because it did not impose its rules. However, it was an extreme and borderline case.

The term *secondary society* covers all other societies. Membership in secondary societies is voluntary, except insofar as the primary society confers, or supports someone conferring, a compulsory aspect. Around us today are a wide variety of secondary societies, the most prominent of which is the family. Churches, businesses, partnerships, clubs, scientific associations, sports teams, hospitals, educational institutions, and religious groups are also examples, and there are a great many others.

Societies often overlap and most people are sensitive to the nuances that define and separate them. In a retail store the management and employees are members of a secondary society, namely, the business. The customers are not members, even when they are in the store, because they are not obligated to follow the set of rules that bind the employees. However, the customers' behavior as well as the behavior of the employees in the store reflects the fact that the customers, the management, the employees, and the business are all members of the primary society and must follow its rules in any case.

Another entity mentioned earlier is the *subsociety*. This is not an independent society, but an organizationally discrete portion of either a primary or a secondary society. Note that a subsociety of a primary society differs from a secondary society that exists in the territory of that primary society. The subsociety of a primary society is a portion of that society and shares its compulsory aspects and its long-range objectives, but differs from other parts of the primary society in having special short-range primary society objectives. The secondary society is a member of the primary society, but has its own independent objectives.

Societal ethics applies to primary societies because these societies are involuntary and can physically compel people in their territories to obey the rules. Personal ethics is the relevant system for the actions of individuals and for the rules of secondary societies in which membership, and thus the obligation to observe the rules, is voluntary.

Another term used earlier is *status society,* which designates a society in which the rules call for all the members to act together for a common objective. As illustrated by the primary society on Ajax Island, this type of society necessarily involves giving each individual member one or more statuses. A status society can be either primary or secondary. Most secondary societies are status societies.

On the other hand, when the members of a society are free to choose their own actions without any obligation to the society to take positive actions, that society will be called a *free society.* Such a society has negative rules that restrict its members' choice of actions but leave each member a sphere in which he or she is free to choose and to act to satisfy desires. A free society can also be either primary or secondary.

The Comet Island society was a primary free society. The rationale of the society was to maximize the value of its members' freedom, a markedly different approach from that of the status society. The fundamental etween these two types of society is that status-society members act as agents of the society whereas free-society members act to satisfy their own personal motives. In the status society, all the responsibility for all the actions belongs to the society. In the free society, all the responsibility for each individual member's action belongs to that member.

The rules of both types of primary society are properly judged by the same societal ethics standard, namely, maximum total good for the people who are direct or indirect members of the primary society. The status society operates on the basis that everyone working together as a team will achieve the greatest total amount of good. The free society operates on the basis that individuals working for their own purposes will achieve the greatest total amount of good. Although the ethical standard is the same for both types of society, some important ethical principles are different, reflecting the different approaches to achieving the standard.

THE FREE SOCIETY

The status society on Ajax Island is a team and the relationship of the members to each other is that of team members. Correspondingly, the free society on Comet Island is a neighborhood and the relationship of the members to each other is that of neighbors. Comet Islanders each know their individual protected spheres of action, which could include real property, personal property, or merely their persons. Usually they are jealous of the boundaries of these spheres. But in the first years the islanders were predominantly law-abiding and did not encroach on their neighbors' spheres.

In contrast to the primary status society, the primary free society has no apparatus for doing things as a society. Consisting of nothing more than members and an agreement obligating the members, the free society has the minimum to qualify it as a society. Even the reaching of the social contract is something outside the society and prior to it. The contract is signed and as a result the society comes into being.

In one sense, the free society is very fragile. It is created by unanimous agreement and can be demolished by one member renouncing the agreement. Of course, the other people can reinstate the society for themselves by making another agreement.

Technically, this is the mechanism by which the members of the Comet Island free society would have punished a criminal. Perhaps the victim would have renounced the agreement, thus destroying the society. Then the population would have reinstated the agreement excluding the criminal. This would have made that individual an outlaw, no longer protected by the rules. Then, it would have been up to the victims or their friends to take revenge on the outlaw. All the action, both the outlawing and the vengeance, would have been taken by individual members acting on their own, not as agents for the society.

The lack of a societal mechanism that could act came up during the invasion of Comet Island by the Babo Islanders. A primary free society has no army, no government, not even a legislature. It is not an acting type of entity.

Of course, many of the situations and functions that we are accustomed to seeing handled by government can be handled by private parties if they are given an opportunity. In the case of defending Comet Island an informal, volunteer militia rose to the occasion. On an everyday basis, there were many typical governmental functions performed privately. Schools were provided, money was issued, messages were carried, and so forth.

On Comet Island most civil disputes in which the participants required help were handled by arbitrators. If the disagreements were too intense for arbitration then a group of neighbors—the more the better—would meet with the disputants and, by the psychology of sheer numbers, dispose of the matter. If a remedy was recommended, it was most likely restitution. Revenge was the alternative remedy and would have required the inconvenient outlawing procedure.

Needless to say, this method of settling disputes was not one that members liked to rely upon. People were careful in dealing with others to make sure the terms of any agreement were clear and, preferably, written. People were also careful not to deal with those they did not trust. Thus, on Comet Island, it was of the utmost importance to have a good reputation and this is one of the hallmarks of a free society.

Modifications of the social contract were arrived at by informal meetings of the members. An official meeting could not be provided for in the agreement, given the insistence by Jake and others that they not be told what to do. But some of the members, as individuals, took it upon themselves to call occasional meetings to renew the agreement.

The Comet Island economy grew rapidly, the primary free society was not constituted to act, and the capacity of lone individuals to get things done was limited; as a result, an increasing proportion of the work was done by secondary status societies. As teams, these secondary status societies usually accomplished substantially more than their members would have working as individuals. There were business teams that operated factories, built ships, sold things in stores, transported goods and people, and did many other things. There were also nonprofit teams that ran the churches, the hospital, the library, a theater, and similar enterprises.

In addition to secondary societies that produced goods and services, there were other secondary societies concerned with distribution of benefits. Some were recreational groups, and not all of them were status societies. The chess club, started by Henry and Seymour, was a secondary free society consisting merely of a set of rules of conduct including a schedule of meetings, and some members who had agreed to the rules.

In the case of a secondary, status-society business the member who owned it chose the objective, usually to satisfy a personal goal such as making money. The employees normally did not participate in choosing the objective, and unlike the situation in a primary status society, the employees' welfare was not a significant part of the objective. Instead, employees contracted with the business to work for wages or salaries, which they then used for their own purposes. Thus each individual's action of working in the business was done for personal motives. However, while at work in the business, as in any status society, the individual acted on behalf of the business as its agent.

RULES IN A FREE SOCIETY

The rules in the Comet Island society were applicable to each of the members in exactly the same way. All members were equal before the law. In a sense all the rules had a general effect. But that didn't mean that the impact of a law on each member was the same. A strong, husky man might not be helped as much by the law against attacking others as a weaker person. The member who didn't own anything worth stealing might not benefit as much by the rule against stealing as would other members. Obviously the impact of a rule on a member influenced his willingness to agree to that rule in the general meeting. However, equalizing the impact of a rule on the members was not an objective, nor was it acceptable to make rules that applied differently to different people.

In like manner, the rules had a disparate impact on the owners and users of various pieces of land. Each piece of land lay a bit differently and that brought with it certain advantages and disadvantages. Actions of certain kinds taken in one location might be illegal because they had an adverse effect on a neighbor, whereas the same action could be taken quite legally on another piece of land where it could have no such effect.

For example, developing a dusty mining operation upwind of residences would create a nuisance, whereas developing one in a remote valley away from neighbors would not. Changing the flow of a stream in a way that cut off neighboring users below would probably be against the rules. A similar change in a place where it would not affect any neighbors might well be legal. In arguing for particular rules, members sought those that would protect uses of their own property and opposed those that would interfere with what they wanted to do.

Nevertheless, the fact that the rules were the same for everyone tended to lead to rules that were reasonably equitable. More important than making them equitable was the fact that, once put into the agreement, each rule persisted and became a feature of the environment of Comet Island like the land and the climate. Members took the impact of the rules into account and made allowance for them in their plans and actions as they did for other features of the environment.

There were other rules, such as traffic rules, whose effects on people were fairly uniform because members were on both sides of the rules at frequent intervals. It might be smoother on the south side of the traffic corridor, but if one weren't on the south side going out, one would likely be coming back.

Other rules about using common property also had reasonably good and general effects on the inhabitants of Comet Island. The rules against polluting or spoiling things applied broadly and produced long-range benefits. There were rules governing cases in which more than one member wanted to use the same portion of the common property at the same time—a particularly good fishing spot for example. There were rules to prevent one member from sitting on a preferred location for too long a time, and rules about using areas of the common property that were so closely adjacent to another area already in use that it would interfere. These latter rules used the concept of "first come first served"—an approach that does not give anybody a permanent advantage—along with the concept of short usage turns where there is competition.

Partly as a result of the unchanging rules, there was constant change in the Comet Island economic environment brought about by the individual decisions and actions of the members. A new shop might spring up across the street from a competitor and a price war would begin. A factory might discover a more efficient way of making a popular product and find that demand was quite elastic. The demand for something another company produced might suddenly soar and then later disappear. A boss might decide to fire an employee. A talented preacher might suddenly appear and attract many new members to his church. Factors of this sort caused uncertainties, but people learned to sense new developments early and were motivated to act in ways that protected themselves.

The overall effect of these changes was to produce more total benefits as seen by the population. Since success in the market dictated the survival and fate of the changes, only those changes that were seen by the consumers as improvements were likely to survive. The fact that the economy grew steadily and quite rapidly was a sign that increasing amounts of tangible benefits were being produced by the system as a whole.

NEGATIVE RULES

The inability of the Comet Island society to function as an entity was due to the fact that it was a creature of negative rules. It takes positive rules, ones that direct people to do things, to confer on a society, whether primary or secondary, the ability to act as a unit. Of course, the way a rule is worded doesn't always reflect its nature. It is the basic sense of the rule that counts. For example, traffic rules, in general, are negative rules. However, one can phrase a traffic rule in a positive way and say "You must drive on the right side of the road." But this would be misleading. The rule is not intended to require that you drive at all. It would be more appropriately worded, "You must not drive on the left side of the road."

Another type of rule that bears some resemblance to a negative rule is the conditional rule composed of (1) a condition and (2) a rule. The condition is negative in its effect: If people refrain from complying with the condition, they don't subject themselves to the rule. If the rule is negative then the conditional rule is negative. If the rule part is positive, the combined effect of the rule is positive or negative depending on the nature of the condition. If the condition is one that a person can readily avoid doing, then the rule is the equivalent of a negative rule not to comply with the condition. If the condition is one that people feel strongly impelled to do, then they must also observe the positive rule, and the effect is positive. A rule that says that if one eats, one must do X is equivalent to a rule that says one must do X. Conditional rules are often used in cases where people would resist a positive rule but are willing to tolerate one if they can avoid it by not triggering the condition. As an example, the rule "You must carry your driver's license when you drive" is clearly conditional because it applies only if you choose to drive. If you choose to drive, however, the rule is a positive one, directing you to carry your driver's license.

Negative rules, on the other hand, present a different problem of ethical optimization. It was pointed out that in the set of positive rules of a status society, the rules interact with each other; the only thing that can be given a value is the overall set of rules. Thus, the value of a proposed rule can only be reliably judged by comparing the value of the whole set of rules, with and without the proposed rule. Negative rules, at least as a first-order approximation, do not interact with each other. Whether a rule that one shall not do X is a good rule does not ordinarily depend on whether there is another rule that one shall not do Y. Thus negative rules can be evaluated incrementally, one by one, with reasonable accuracy.

Andrew's assumption was that the most effective way to benefit members was through an all-powerful society. The underlying assumption embodied in the system on Comet Island was just the opposite, namely, that individuals were their own best agents for making progress toward their ultimate purposes. For this type of program to work well, everyone has to act in accordance with their personal motives to accomplish the things they want done.

The free society does not obligate individuals to decide what would be best for society or other people, as is done in classical utilitarianism. Rather, it relies on individuals to make their own choices for their own personal good or that of such others as they may choose.

The people on Comet Island didn't spend much time theorizing about ethics; they probably picked up their ideas about the ethical standard in discussions with the managers on Ajax Island. Unlike the situation on Ajax Island, the total-good standard was not directly involved in day-to-day planning on Comet Island, but was used in the arguments for and against proposed rules.

The drafting of the agreement on Comet Island was conducted as a bargaining session in which members looked out for their own interests, bearing in mind their indirect interest in seeing neighbors solve their own problems. While trying to get what they wanted, they were cautious about rules that would mistreat someone, because such rules might establish a precedent that could later victimize them. On some issues, such as the rule not to physically attack one another, most members agreed without much discussion. On others, such as whether creating smoke that blew over onto a neighbor's land constituted an interference with private property, there was more argument.

There were several fundamental principles that have been mentioned and were observed. The first was to make the rules uniformly applicable to every member of the society. This is a normal feature of a negative-rule system, since there is no mechanism for selecting members and giving them special status. This would require positive actions by the society or the writing of such status into the rules. No such mechanism was likely to be added to the rules in a free-bargaining process requiring unanimity. In addition, making a rule apply to everyone tended to open up the benefits to as broad a range of members as possible.

A second fundamental principle was to avoid changing the rules once they were agreed upon. Having the rules uniformly applicable helps level the playing field. Avoiding changes in the rules assumes the playing field will never be entirely level and that it is more important for players planning their actions to be able to learn its contours and to be able to rely on the field holding its shape.

These principles also restrained people from writing rules whose range of application would be too specific. A rule to prevent people from using their land for a cattle feed lot because of the smell, for example, would be rejected in favor of a more general rule restricting a landowner from imposing too much odor on his neighbors, assuming that rule was justified.

Finally, it was important in the free society for all members to know all of the rules they were supposed to obey. Participation in passing the rules and signing the agreement that listed them were important steps that helped to impress the whole range of rules on everyone. Keeping the rules logical and minimizing their number were also important considerations. Even more important was the attention that members of a free society give to the rules because they define each individual's sphere of choice. This is quite different from the situation in a status society, where the only rules individuals really need to know are the particular rules that govern their respective actions, minute by minute. They can be counseled by a supervisor if they have any doubts.

7

Theory

STATUS SOCIETIES AND FREE SOCIETIES

Both the Ajax Island and Comet Island societies prospered in the first years of their existence. Their respective members were happy and looked forward to a future in which the good things they had been experiencing would continue. The two societies had many things in common. They raised the same crops, ate the same kinds of foods, wore similar clothing, and doctored themselves with the same medicines. They used the same tools and technologies and went through the same steps to build habitations and develop land for farming. A casual observer might have taken both of them to be ordinary English colonial settlements.

But underneath the similarities, these two societies operated in markedly different ways. On Ajax Island, the members followed set routines; worked at all times in a cooperative, disciplined way; and were completely unselfish and free of personal motives in their actions. On Comet Island, members did whatever they individually decided to do, were only cooperative and disciplined when they wanted to be, and were often quite selfish in their actions.

Historically, there have been a few societies rather like these. There have been, and probably still are, isolated monasteries that operate on a scheme reasonably close to that used in a status society. Some societies operating on a scheme reasonably close to that used in free societies have existed in Scandinavia and on the frontier in the United States. However, societies of either type have a tendency to be short-lived and not able to cope with a normal range of population.

The same ethical standard can be used to evaluate the overall accomplishments of the Ajax Island and Comet Island societies—the total good achieved by all the members. By this standard, they were both successful. Both used sound approaches to develop their respective sets of rules, approaches that were consistent with their respective sets of ethical principles. However, in many respects these were opposite approaches to the problem of conducting a good society.

One indication of a successful society, present in both Ajax and Comet rules, is undivided responsibility. This means that under the rules of the society the party that has the authority to act will bear the direct consequences. On Comet Island this is clear enough: members chose their actions and prospered or suffered thereby. Undivided responsibility on Ajax Island arose from the fact that the members both acted and bore the consequences as agents for the society. It was the society that ultimately chose the actions and bore the consequences. If members were injured, they suffered as agents of society; the corresponding detriment would be subtracted in an evaluation of the total good achieved.

It is significant that each of the societies had a fairly narrow range of members. A good many of the members, certainly the leaders, of the society on Ajax Island were intellectually inclined and had chosen to submit to the discipline of a rigorous set of rules in order to live an ordered life that emphasized the activity they desired most, philosophical discussion. A good many of the members, certainly the leaders, of the society on Comet Island were men of integrity and responsibility. They kept every promise, obeyed every rule, and took full responsibility for their own lives and for their families without expecting help beyond that which other members might volunteer as individuals. It was also significant that both islands were located in a remote corner of the Pacific Ocean and were not threatened by the acquisitive nations of Europe or elsewhere.

Obviously the select membership and the freedom from threat of outside interference could not continue for long; nor would one expect to find either in any sovereign state today. Under normal circumstances, it seems clear that neither of these approaches to writing the rules could produce a stable sovereign state that would persist.

There appear to be only two fundamental approaches for a primary society to set up desirable rules. The societies on Ajax and Comet islands each used only one of them. They were thus prototypical extreme societies rather than practical long-term models and differed substantially from the sovereign states of today.

But all sovereign states resemble both of these societies in varying degrees. One could no doubt construct a scale with these two extreme societies at either end of the spectrum and characterize particular existing sovereign states as positioned somewhere between, some perhaps closer to one extreme and some to the other. However, it is more useful to consider the factors that produce this effect.

The reason that sovereign states resemble these prototypical societies is that all states are constructed of rules. Rules are discrete entities and have distinguishing characteristics. The types of obligations defined by the rules used in the two island societies were opposites in several respects. Fundamentally, a particular rule of a sovereign state either supports the government, i.e., its agents, in choosing what to do, or supports individual private citizens in making their own choices. A rule either obligates the government or citizens to do something positive or it leaves the citizens free to choose their own course of action within limits defined by it and other obligations. A rule is either a positive or negative obligation in its basic impact.

All the rules of a sovereign state can be analyzed in terms of these two types. Each rule may be viewed as based on the status-society or the free-society approach to setting up the relationships in a society. The two sets of rules seem to be mutually exclusive, although there may be combinations, such as some of the conditional rules. Both types of rules, if they are in accordance with ethical principles, are intended to lead to the same objective—that given by the standard. As a result, they also have some points of similarity, such as placing as much value on good for one member of society as on good for any other.

As a practical matter, mixing the two types of rules is like mixing oil and water; what results is an oil-in-water emulsion or a water-in-oil emulsion. One or the other is usually the continuous phase, and if that is not the case, the mixture is not very desirable. The rule system of most healthy sovereign states rests on a foundation composed mainly of a network of either status-society or free-society rules. In the first case, the rules in this foundation are written so that the government takes fundamental responsibility for the welfare of its citizens or perhaps so that the citizens are required to support the government in achieving societal goals. These status-society systems have priority over all the citizens' individual choices and projects. In the second case, the citizens have responsibility for their own welfare and they have rights that will prevail against the government in many cases. In such systems the basic negative rules operate in the absence of specific rules to the contrary. In the United States, the underlying network is composed of free-society rules that contemplate citizens being responsible for themselves and making their own choices.

As long as a society adds mainly rules that are of the same type as those in its foundation network, writing optimum rules is relatively simple. The society can readily achieve a system of rules that produces undivided responsibility. Usually, however, states introduce a substantial group of rules of the opposite type into their systems. It is sometimes possible to do this without substantial friction between the underlying-network rules and those of the opposite type. Undivided responsibility can then be largely preserved.

In many other cases, however, opposite-type rules are introduced that conflict with the functioning of the underlying-network rules. Responsibility may then become divided. A system of mixed rules may easily get so complicated that people lose sight of how the overall system should operate. Following the wrong ethical principles, they introduce rules that are plainly ill-advised. For example, the obligation to pay taxes is a status-society type of rule and can be carried to extremes following status-society principles. Unfortunately, at high rates taxes are a well-established mechanism for interfering with the underlying-network free-society rules that protect the free-society markets.

Likewise, the introduction of an opposite-type rule may fail to produce the benefit expected because of conflicts with the foundation rules. For example, rules intended to introduce private enterprise into a status society may be ineffective if the activities are still subject to the regulators that manage the other status-society parts of the state.

One of the uses of ethical principles should be to guide us toward a set of rules that will work together without interfering with each other. As illustrated by the operation of rules on Ajax and Comet islands, the ethical principles for status-society rules differ from those for free-society rules. In applying ethical principles to the rules of a real state, one must choose which set to apply. It depends on which kind of rule is being considered. So, the first step in a mixed-rule state is to identify, by type, each of the relevant rules.

Interestingly, most individuals seem to think naturally in terms of, and feel most comfortable with, either the status-society or free-society rules. One might guess that people get these attitudes more from their everyday experience with secondary societies than with their primary one. This dichotomy can be seen in people's choices of terminology and the solutions to problems that spring to their minds. These inherent, opposing preferences are probably one reason so many people who engage in political arguments reflect a real lack of understanding of the opposing viewpoint.

For example, nearly everyone believes that all members of a society deserve equal treatment by the government. To a person who thinks in terms of a free-society, negative-rule framework, this means that the laws should be applied exactly the same to all members, depending only on their behavior. To a person who thinks in terms of a status-society, positive-rule framework, equal treatment means that members should be assigned to the class they deserve to be in and that all members of the class should be treated alike.

FREE-SOCIETY VERSUS STATUS-SOCIETY RULES

The following is a list of some characteristics that bear on the identity of a primary-society rule.

	Free Society	**Status Society**
Rule Type	Negative	Positive
Rule Applicability	Uniform	By status
Member's Role	Principal	Agent
Responsibility	Member	Society
Type of Action	Selfish	Unselfish
Relationship	Neighbors	Team mates

Looking to see whether a rule is positive or negative provides a good indication of whether it is a free-society or status-society rule. However, given the variety of ways in which a rule can be worded, one must look at the meaning rather than merely the form of the rule. A positive rule is one that requires positive action by someone. Any action taken by the government reflects the existence of a positive rule.

A reference to status in the rule is a strong indication that it is of the status-society type. Rules that apply uniformly to everyone's actions and do not include class designations based on elements other than actions, are typically free-society rules. Traffic rules are typical free-society rules that apply to everyone who chooses to go onto a public street. Welfare-recipient entitlements are typical status-society rules that apply only to members who have been given special status by the government based on their circumstances (rather than on their actions).

A rule often indicates the type of roles members are to fill. If it is a free-society rule, it does not apply, except to prevent members from choosing to take illegal actions. In status-society rules the government or a member is required to do something. The member in this case and of course the government are thus agents of society. Rules that forbid people to pollute are examples of free-society rules. Those that require people to clean up something are status-society rules.

Normally, the rule also implies the party that is responsible. In a free-society rule, members are assumed to be responsible for themselves. Status-society rules are part of a program in which society has the overall responsibility for the members and they are required to follow the directions of society. A requirement that a member or the government maintain a marshland for bird nesting is a status-society rule, which implies that the government has assumed responsibility for the welfare of the birds. The rule that individuals refrain from shooting birds is a free-society rule.

In the case of a free-society rule, members are free to act selfishly on their own behalf or on the basis of any other personal motive without an obligation to take the welfare of society into account. In acting on a status-society rule, members, even those receiving a benefit, act in accordance with their obligations to society. In a free society a person's lawful behavior is considered his or her own business, while in a status society, members must act to discharge their civic duties.

From the underlying nature of the rule, it may be clear that members are assumed either to be working together as a team or to be working on their own as neighbors. A government program giving out food stamps is a status-society feature in which society tries to take care of needy members, a typical teamwork objective. The right to spend the food stamps as the recipient desires is a free-society idea in which the recipient chooses his or her own actions.

Whether a rule belongs in one category or the other and whether it is in accordance with relevant ethical principles, are two different questions. Rules that are not in accordance with ethical principles are more difficult to classify; some of the tests listed above assume that the rule is in line with principle. For example, a rule that discriminates between members on the basis of race is a status-society rule because it is based on status, but is not in accordance with either status-society or free-society principles. Most rules intended for the benefit of a dictator rather than the whole society are also status-society rules, but they, too, are generally not in accordance with either status-society or free-society principles.

Legislatures, the idea of majority rule, and the idea that it is proper for interest groups to seek rules that will benefit them are all derived from the free society. Money is a free-society feature, although the idea that it should be a government monopoly comes from the status society. A foundation of free-society rules in a primary society usually results in a free-enterprise economy and a business apparatus that utilizes secondary status societies to handle much of the day-to-day operations.

The major features of government, other than the legislature, are derived from the status society. The executive functions seem to be descended from the production department, and the judicial functions from the distribution department. Taxes, a ubiquitous feature of states, come from the status society. All the other things that the government runs—the army, the police, the schools, etc.—are status-society features. Licensing, permits, and the like are examples of status-society rules imposed on free-society activities.

ETHICAL PRINCIPLES

In the morality system ethical principles are essentially the same as ethical rules. Both are duties that should be observed, although the principles may be the more abstract or general ones. In a consequentialist system, such as the one used here, there does not appear to be a comparable function. Thus *ethical principles* as used here means some generalizations that provide good advice in selecting rules. They function in a way comparable to the "principles of good management" that one might learn in a business school. Ethical principles in this sense constitute a broad subject, one that I cannot claim to have explored very much. The following discussion is intended to cover a few of the principles that seem evident.

Perhaps the first principle is that a society should use its best efforts to formulate rules that maximize good for all its members. In the case of the status society this would be done in a coordinated management effort aimed directly at that result. In the case of the free society there is no comparable entity that can aim directly at the result. It must come out of a legislative process. Given that the legislative process inherently reflects people trying to arrive at rules that will benefit themselves individually, the best rules probably result when the legislators are most successful in accomplishing their long-range purpose. Normally legislators seem to place too much emphasis on short-range direct benefits; the need is rather to give adequate weight to the indirect and long-range effects of the rules.

Proposed rules should be examined to see if they are consistent with appropriate ethical principles. The benefits and detriments should be appraised. Modifications of the rule should be considered to see whether other versions might be better. Taking everything into account, the rule should show a predominance of benefit to justify its adoption. This type of routine would be done formally in a status society and would be the justification given in the arguments by members in the legislative meeting of a free society.

In the free society, since the functioning of the society depends on the actions initiated by individual members to achieve the good they want, the rules operate by creating an environment in which members can exploit the assets in their sphere of choice without fearing direct interference. For the most part, the rules protect members from direct, violent physical intervention, appropriation of their property, or damage from agents such as pollutants in the water or air. An extension of this concept also prohibits intervention by fraud.

However, it is important in the free society that the rules not restrict indirect interference with other people, since that would unduly curtail basic freedoms. Indirect interference means actions taken to achieve some benefit for the actor that have an indirect, detrimental effect on someone else. (Actions that result in physical interference with other parties or their property, even though that is not the main purpose of the action, are forms of direct interference.) Competition is the normal form of indirect interference: for example, company A indirectly deprives company B of a sale by offering a better price.

In a free society, it is important to have the rules apply to everyone alike. There should be no consideration of status; all should be free to pursue their own purposes as effectively as their resources permit. This principle also argues against rules that are so specific they apply only to a few cases. It is better to write broad rules that reflect a general underlying distinction.

The free society depends on the market to allocate benefits, since it lacks the bureaucratic allocation mechanism of the status society. Thus, any scarce resource should be private property, potentially on the market, rather than common property. The latter should be restricted to things that can be used freely by everyone, subject to protective rules and conventions.

The free society achieves good by giving all members a chance to do what they wish. Consequently, there should be no restrictions against behavior that is merely thought by society to be objectionable or ill-advised, rather than harmful to others. This means that speech, travel, assembly, trading, contracts of all sorts, enterprises, and so forth should not generally be restricted.

Promises are an important mechanism in the functioning of a free society and there should be rules against breaking them. By the same token, there should be a rule against lying to other people, especially in circumstances where harm can result.

It is important that the rules, particularly those having to do with property, not change very often, so that people can take rules into account in making long-range plans.

The free society depends on its members' using their initiative, which requires that they know the rules. This in turn makes it important that the rules be few in number and simple to understand; there should not be a lot of unnecessary or marginally important rules for everyone to remember. The rules that are in force should be adequately communicated to all members at reasonable intervals.

Note that this is very different from the status society, where people are told what to do. In a status society there are a great many rules and the short-range ones, at least, need to be changed frequently to achieve optimum results. Since individual members need to know only what they specifically are to do and are not permitted to initiate their own actions, knowing the rules beyond those that apply immediately to them is not needed. However, there is, correspondingly, a responsibility for the government to adequately inform each member of the actions he or she is obligated to take.

The status society operates by providing members directly with benefits of various sorts. Unlike the free society, a status society allocates benefits in a way that bears some resemblance to dividing a pie; an extra portion for one person is taken away from the benefits going to others. This is understandable given that status-society operations involve members' acting as agents of society rather than seeking to satisfy personal motives.

One aspect of the status society is the need to assign members to classes for various purposes. The definition of the status or class, and the choice of which members belong in it, must be objective and related to the purpose of the operation and in any case should be governed by the need to optimize total good. Value judgments should be explicitly covered in the major written rules so that managers who administer the rules on a day-to-day basis will not be called on to make such judgments themselves, but only to reach factual conclusions.

MIXING FREE-SOCIETY AND STATUS-SOCIETY RULES

The two kinds of rules result in two different types of societies and are based on entirely different approaches to the problem of maximizing good for everyone. It is nearly always the case that a society better than either of the prototypical ones could, on the face of it, be constructed by incorporating desirable features from both into society rules. To a limited extent the two types of rules can be mixed without substantial problems by (1) careful choice of compatible rules, and (2) observing the ethical principles appropriate to the types of rules involved.

Unfortunately, this isn't easy and it is not often accomplished. As an example, consider the systems used for the punishment of criminals in sovereign states that employ an underlying free-society rule network. Typically, punishment is primarily retribution, which is based on the idea that the criminal action has injured society. This idea is taken from the status-society mechanism where it makes sense, given that the individual's responsibility is directly to that society.

However, the victims of the crime do not fare the same in mixed-rule societies. The status society would rush benefits to the members who are injured by the crime because they would be in a condition where they could make excellent use of benefits. This part of the system is usually not imported into the mixed-rule state. Instead, the victim is left to his or her free-society option, restitution, which is frequently worthless, since the state gets its punishment in first. The victim is not allowed to engage in the other free-society option, revenge, because it is forbidden in the status-society view of rules.

Apparently because people do not understand that they are dealing with two political approaches, they select rules from both and patch them together without providing the offsets and balances that exist in the pure systems.

As another example, a status-society distribution feature—welfare—is often added to a free-society network of rules. In the pure status society, benefits are monitored to make sure they are used properly in order to get optimum results. The problem in a mixed society is that this part of the system is omitted so as to preserve welfare recipients' free-society rights to do what they please in their protected spheres of choice, which are assumed now to include the welfare benefits. The good that is accomplished may thus be considerably less than it would be in a status society.

There is a further fundamental difficulty with introducing status-society rules into a society that is based on a network of free-society rules. Introducing a major segment of the status-society rules can substantially diminish the efficacy of the free-society rules. Careful drafting of the rules can minimize this interference, but it becomes difficult to achieve as the proportion of status-society rules grows beyond a certain point. Introducing free-society rules into a status society is probably even more disruptive to the fundamental rule network of that society. In both cases, societies that are not predominantly one or the other are likely to have divided responsibility and to contain a substantial portion of rules that do not follow the principles of societal ethics.

8

Rights, Obligations, and Responsibilities

RIGHTS VERSUS OBLIGATIONS

The rules created by a society have two complementary aspects: rights and obligations. While they are not necessarily opposites, people concerned with one of these aspects of a rule often take positions in opposition to those concerned with the other.

The relationship of the two aspects is evident in a status society. Members of the society are obligated to do for the society that which is required by the rules: for example, work of various sorts or the utilizing of benefits society has provided them. Society, thereby, has a right to the positive performance of the members. The rules also obligate society to do positive things for its members: confer various benefits, for example. The members have, thereby, rights to the benefits.

The situation in a prototypical free society is different. Obligations are not to the society, but to other members. The social contract is between members, not between the members and society. The obligation not to steal, for example, is an obligation owed to members who own property. The purpose of the rules is to enhance the value of members' spheres of choice, the ones in which members can do what they choose.

One might compare a member's sphere of choice to a house. A house is constructed of boards and beams and panes of glass, etc. A builder necessarily thinks in terms of such entities while cutting the lumber to size, nailing it together, etc., until the house is finished. The boards and beams and panes of glass (that is to say, the pieces that compose the house) are analogous to the obligations in a free society (the pieces that compose the system of rules) which, in turn, define and protect the spheres of choice.

But boards and beams and panes of glass are not what the salespeople refer to when they describe the house to prospective buyers. They are not the terms in which buyers will view the house as they live in it. Instead, they will largely view the house in terms of how it affects them, how they can utilize it, and how many things they can do in it. They think of the house in terms of the rooms, the halls, and the capabilities of the appliances. These elements are analogous to the features of one's sphere of choice in a free society which, in turn, reflect one's rights in a system of negative rules.

Rights are what the beneficiaries see in a set of rules. In a free society the rules protect people from interference by others as they utilize the capabilities in themselves and their property. Rules do not give a member the right to receive positive, beneficial actions the way rules do in a status society.

SENSE OF OBLIGATION

As with many ordinary words, "rule" designates several kinds of thing: for example, a rule of thumb for how long it takes to drive home from work, or a personal rule that one will stop drinking after the third drink. But in our discussion here, when a society is defined as based on a set of rules, the term is being used in a narrow sense to denote an *obligation* to perform or not perform an action.

In this context "obligation" has two different but related meanings. First, it may designate a certain type of thought existing in the obliger's mind. This will be called a *sense of obligation.* Second, it may imply a societal configuration, designed so that it is in a member's best interest to act in a certain way. This will be called an *organizational obligation.* Many definitions of "obligation" use rather high-level abstractions. The intention here is to extract a tangible physical essence from the word.

Whether someone has a particular sense of obligation is known only to that person, although others may well have an accurate idea of its existence from observing the person's actions or spoken intentions. The mechanism for arriving at the sense of obligation seems to involve language. Like language, the sense of obligation appears to be something unique to humans. We have, as do other animate beings, mechanisms such as needs, pains, emotions, perceptions, etc., for arriving at the choices we choose as best. Unlike other animate beings, humans have in the sense of obligation a mechanism for choosing what to do, that is an alternative to the mechanisms for choosing the best.

The sense of obligation is the mental entity that accompanies a promise one has made and intends to keep. An example might be a promise to obey the rules of a society.

To pursue this a little further, the sense of obligation seems to be in the nature of a plan one has for future action. If one promises to do something, one plans to do it. But it is not a simple plan. Rather, there is a double plan involved in a sense of obligation. One part is the plan to carry out or refrain from carrying out an action in accordance with a promise. The other is the plan to keep alive the first plan and not be diverted from it by the opportunity to instead do something that turns out to be more attractive.

Plan is used here in the broad sense of aiming at a goal when one initiates an action. For instance, one must have a plan in order to pick up the telephone when it rings. A plan in this sense is roughly equivalent to an intention.

In a person with a healthy psychology, creation of the sense of obligation is a conscious, volitional act. Even though it occurs only in the mind, it is an act of the same general nature as any other purposeful act and is done because it is something the person thinks is best. Creating a sense of obligation requires making some of the decisions that would be made if the person were to do the act immediately. A sense of obligation is not something created by a mere feeling or perception, although those may be involved. It requires the use of concepts.

If the purpose is merely to take advantage of an expected opportunity, then it would be easy enough to formulate a simple plan that could be laid aside when it came time to act in case something better had come up. Logically, there must be a reason to commit oneself to a promise, to a sense of obligation rather than adopt a simple plan. If action is taken on the basis of external objectives (as opposed merely to satisfying some internal psychological need), a benefit can be obtained from committing to the sense of obligation only if that obligation is communicated to another person. Another person must be persuaded that a promise is being made that would justify him or her providing a benefit in return. Thus, making promises is logically an external or public act that involves communication.

This is not to deny that people make promises silently to themselves, perhaps as a form of discipline. One might doubt that such mental exercises create the sense of obligation that an exchange of promises with another person would.

There are aberrations. Many techniques have been developed to lead people to assume a sense of obligation without offering them real benefits. One technique avoids asking for promises, but concentrates on persuading people that they already have obligations. The extent to which such ploys are successful may be judged by the degree to which people suffer pangs of guilt in circumstances where they have not, in fact, broken a promise.

The sense of obligation is the mechanism used in the operation of the primary free society because the organizational obligation mechanism is not available to a significant extent in that society. The social contract procedure, on the face of it, creates a sense of obligation by having the members bargain to an agreement with each one formally promising the group to obey the rules.

ORGANIZATIONAL OBLIGATION

Let's look at another situation. It is evening. Mother reminds nine-year-old Dennis to take his bath. Dennis knows he is supposed to bathe; it's a family rule and he definitely has the obligation to take a bath now. But Dennis has no sense of obligation about taking a bath. If he can get away with skipping the bath, he will do so with feelings of elation rather than guilt. But when his mother reminds him, Dennis knows he'd better do it. If he doesn't, she will haul him upstairs, dump him into the bathtub, and add a little punishment of some sort to provide deterrence.

Dennis's family is predominantly a status society (although most families use a mixture of status-society and free-society rules with more of the latter demanded by teenagers) and his taking the bath is an organizational obligation. Dennis's obligation to tell the truth was originally an organizational obligation, but his parents have persuaded him to adopt a sense of obligation to tell the truth. It is likely that, as he leaves the family and ventures out into the world, Dennis will recognize telling the truth as usually a good policy from considerations of personal ethics. That may undercut his sense of obligation on this subject, or may persuade him that it is a good practice to leave in place.

An organizational obligation is created when a society arranges appropriate punishments (or incentives) for the breaking of (or abiding by) the rules. This is the normal basis on which people pay their taxes, serve in the army when drafted, and discharge many other obligations the government imposes, as well as the basis on which many people do their jobs. This is to say that people discharge these legal obligations largely because of concern for what society or their employer might do to them if they don't.

The organizational obligation does not require any particular state of mind; nor does it require consent by members for them to be bound or that they know the rule. Ignorance of the rule is no excuse, although it may be evidence of a poorly run society.

The organizational obligation is characteristic of the primary status society. It does not require integrity or good intentions. Thus, the status-society rules are adapted to members with a wide range of characteristics and motivations. Note that it relies on the members' regular decision-making systems, and is based on the idea that members will do what they feel is best for them.

Despite all the advantages of the organizational obligation, the other mechanism, the sense of obligation, is a more efficient, less expensive way to get people to do things. Even status societies will get as much obedience as they can by using the sense of obligation on top of the organizational obligation.

The organizational obligation is also a feature of secondary status societies. In a business, for example, promotions, salary levels, maintenance of employment, etc., all depend on employees following the rules. However, secondary societies are voluntary, the employees usually promise to obey the rules and the managers often fondly assume that the sense of obligation is the factor that motivates employees' actions.

RIGHTS

Although the system of rules is made up of obligations, people, especially those in a free society, are mostly concerned on a day-to-day basis with their rights. Rights in a free society are a major factor in determining the scope of the sphere of choice people have. People are constantly choosing, are very sensitive to limitations on their choices, and thus are very sensitive to any encroachment on their rights, just as they are to anything else that increases or reduces the size or value of their spheres of choice.

In brief, rights are other people's obligations. This includes rights in the form of options. In these cases, the holder of the right may trigger somebody else's obligation at the holder's choice. Part of members' contacts with government involve the exercise of options and the receipt of government benefits, such as direct subsidies, delivery of letters through the post, or shelter under a license law for proposed activities.

There are exceptions. Sometimes there is a rule that obliges members to do something that is believed to be for their own individual benefit. Obviously, an obligation for a motorcycle rider to wear a helmet does not confer a corresponding right. The government may be a minor and indirect beneficiary of such rules, but for the most part, this kind of rule seems to be an example of creation of rightless obligations.

Because of the way we use our knowledge of rights and the strong emotions we attach to them, we forget at times that they are only the obverse of obligations. People, especially in politics, sometimes act as though rights are something they can create directly by announcement. Typically the phrase "right to life, liberty, and the pursuit of happiness" sketches a fine goal, but it only becomes a right insofar as it is the obverse of a corresponding set of obligations. Too often, proposed rights, like proposed floor plans, are merely incident to a sales pitch.

It is important to cast political proposals in terms obligations. Rights may be something that cannot be constructed or would cost too much. Discussing the features of a system of rules in terms of obligations makes clear the practical and theoretical problems involved.

It should not be forgotten, however, that the motive for the obligation is usually the right. The reason the house is built is that somebody wants to live in that kind of structure.

RESPONSIBILITY

The word "responsibility" is often used to mean answerable. Personal responsibility is invoked in cases of action or inaction to indicate whether an individual deserves praise or blame. The word is used here with a slightly different meaning. *Responsibility* here means (1) having and (2) using the authority to choose an action, (3) taking the action, and (4) bearing the consequences of having taken the action.

In the free society, members have the authority to make choices and act accordingly. They bear the consequences of their actions, although others are usually affected by the action, too. In the status society, the society chooses the actions and bears the consequences. Thus the responsibility is undivided in both, as discussed earlier.

In a system of divided responsibility, the authority and the taking of action is in the hands of one party, while the direct consequences are borne by another. A rule system that has divided responsibility is not necessarily at odds with ethical principles, but undivided responsibility seems to be an indication of ethically desirable rules.

In many small decisions—the chocolate or vanilla choices—people cannot bring much in the way of reason to bear. It is difficult to write down rules for how such decisions should be made, or make good choices for somebody else. Such decisions are likely to be based on emotion, which doesn't necessarily mean they are unimportant or ill-advised. But clearly the people who bear the consequences are in a much better position in such cases to make the optimum choices. Even in decisions that are more susceptible to rational analysis, experience tells us that, other things being equal, the best choices are usually made by the people who bear the consequences. One of the problems people have with bureaucrats in government or business is the poor quality of their decisions. This may be due to several factors, but it seems to correlate with the fact that the bureaucrats do not bear the consequences of the decisions they make, except in indirect ways.

There are ways to improve such situations. Setting up a formal method to measure the success of a decision usually permits one to construct a parallel set of consequences that can be used to motivate the decision maker, a bonus for example. Such consequences might be called *collateral consequences*.

An interesting approach is used by professions. The client, who will bear the consequences of the action, is not generally qualified to do the job; undivided responsibility is thus not a reasonable goal. Professionals, whether barbers or physicians, go through a special course of training in a narrow field. As part of this, they are taught not to make decisions for clients outside the field of their profession. Included in the training is a methodology for determining what is best for the client and a procedure for accomplishing it. The activity is rational and critically reviewed by other professionals. On top of this, there are usually collateral consequences to motivate the professionals.

9

A Constitution

Henry looked around the room: at the fireplace with the piglet on the spit, at the plankwood walls, at the rafters and the ladder running up to the loft. He sniffed the luscious scent of hot roast pork in the air. A deep sense of accomplishment and pleasure came over him, comparing his home to the hut he had lived in originally.

He smiled fondly, glancing across at Nora, who was standing near the fireplace preparing dinner. She had been the most important factor in the changes. He had found her hiding in a bush after the invasion three years before. She looked very frightened sitting there, pushing her two little boys behind her, and he respected the stubborn way she shielded them. Smiling, he offered her food. He had been patient and finally she followed him home. She had been a really good wife and had done more than her share of the work. And the boys were doing well. Nora had insisted that they learn English and the other things Henry taught them.

As he watched, Nora looked over at the crib where their four-month-old baby daughter lay asleep. Responsibility for a wife and children, Henry reflected, was a powerful force motivating him to improve life on the island.

The house was small: just one room with a bed at one end, a table and chairs at the other, and a sleeping loft above. To pay for the lumber, Henry had sold a piece of land. He still had plenty of land left, although there were now three men on the island who had more.

Henry heard a noise outside and walked over to look through a little glass window in the door. It was Seymour, the first of his guests, shuffling up the path to the house, wearing his characteristic disappointed expression. Smiling, Henry opened the door. "Hello Seymour, come in, come in."

Seymour was a large homely man with frizzled hair, grey eyes, and a long, plain face. He finally grinned as they shook hands. Then he sat down on one of the chairs and let his face relax back into its normal expression.

A few minutes later, Hermann and Big Joe arrived together. Hermann was a stocky German with a neatly trimmed black beard and a business-like expression, the seriousness of which was offset by the twinkle in his eye. He was the most progressive of the merchants and clearly the leader of the principal village, located on the harbor at the south end of the island.

Big Joe was quite different: a very large Irishman with black hair, blue eyes, and a jovial manner which gave the impression that everything he said was meant to be taken humorously. He had hands like small hams, with the rest of him in proportion. Acknowledging Henry's hand waving him to the sturdiest chair, Big Joe took the several steps slowly, stooping, with his hand in front of his forehead to protect it from hitting a rafter. He reached the chair and sank into it with a sigh. The chair creaked.

The four men sat around the table talking idly, glancing occasionally at the fireplace. Their minds were not yet on the subject of their meeting. Finally, Nora took the spit off the fire, put the roast piglet on a wooden platter, and put it down on the table in front of the men. Each man hitched his chair up to the table and carved off a piece of the roast pork with his knife. "It's fabulous," said Big Joe. "She's put herbs or something on it."

Henry said, "I suppose. I've told her I like it, and she always makes it the same way."

When Hermann finished his third large piece of pork he leaned back in his chair and smiled. "Delicious," he said, in his thick accent. "I'll bet living here is better than it was when you were alone." Henry rolled his eyes but kept on eating. "On the other hand," said Herman, "maybe you sometimes wish the rest of us would go away and let you lead the simple life again."

Henry swallowed and grinned. "No, I enjoy the comforts. And I'll put up with the rest of you to get them." Nora brought over a bowl of taro and Henry patted her affectionately as she turned to go back.

After filling themselves on the pork and taro, the men edged their chairs back a bit and started on a tray of fruit. Henry said, "Getting the women here made a world of difference. I'd still be living in the hut, and you probably wouldn't have brought your wife and settled here with us at all, Hermann."

"Yes, I'm sure the place would have had a different character if you hadn't found wives." Hermann said.

"You originally settled here to start a tannery?" said Seymour, looking over at Hermann.

"No, not exactly," Hermann said. "I originally came over to buy pigskin after a sample of it showed up in Santiago. The pigskin was superb. And then I saw the island and liked the way it ran. Besides that, it was obvious there would never be much of that pigskin produced unless I came over and organized the business."

"I don't know that side of the story," said Seymour. "What did you do?"

"I went out and got farmers to plant maize, catch pigs, and start raising them in pens. Some of it took a little capital, which I had to bring in. When enough pigs were available, I built that slaughterhouse and tannery by the stream on the west side. You probably know, we ship out the best pigskin in the world, and quite a variety of pickled pork products."

"And you make your own vinegar and ships, too," said Henry.

"Yes, originally for our own use, but by now we sell the majority of it to others," said Hermann.

Seymour muttered, "I guess it never hurts to have a captive market when you're starting."

Nora stood before them holding a tray of cups. "Ohelo wine. It's a specialty of my people." She handed out the cups and the men leaned back and sipped the wine. They nodded at each other in approval. As they relaxed, Henry's mind wandered back to the attack a month earlier, the event that had prompted this evening meeting.

Henry was standing in one of the groups on the edge of the village watching the ship tack into the harbor. It was midafternoon and the sun was bright, but there were storm clouds in the distance. At first, Henry thought the ship had misjudged, come in too far, and would run aground. But he could see sailors measuring the depth of the water, and at the last moment the ship dropped anchor. It was a warship. He could see the guns behind the ports. He'd guessed as much when the ship was first sighted, and had sent word asking the men who lived nearby to gather and bring their rifles.

Twice in the last year, warships had come by to pay a visit. Reports of the island's prosperity must have been getting around. Both captains had behaved politely; apparently neither had any orders to be aggressive. But both had suggested that, as a safety measure, the island might wish to be annexed as a colony of the ship's mother country. Henry, acting as an unofficial head of state, had declined, but he got the impression that the group of armed men standing around behind him had probably been the factor that persuaded the captains not to press the matter.

Henry looked up at a knoll above the village. About fifty men with rifles had assembled there in the trees. He thought he could see Big Joe moving among them and relaxed a little. Big Joe had years of experience fighting in several armies and was a military leader everyone respected.

Henry looked back at the ship. It was swinging slowly around. Gradually it came broadside to the village and dropped another anchor. The portholes were open, the guns had been run out and there were men beside them. The ship looked sloppy and it had still not raised a flag.

Suddenly, puffs of white smoke appeared across the side of the ship. Henry threw up his arm instinctively and at the same instant heard the thunder, the swishing of cannon balls, and the crashing all around him as they tore into buildings. Henry was stunned. The nearest building had a caved-in wall. He ran in to see if anyone was hurt. There was no one inside.

The building beside it was untouched, but the next building was damaged. He saw two men carrying another out of the wreckage and rushed to help. There were more crashes and the roar of another volley. Henry looked at the ship and could see a pirate flag. The ship was launching three boats. He glanced up at the men on the knob. They had disappeared.

"Get out!" he shouted. "Everyone get out of the village. Run up into the woods!" People scattered, running in all directions like ants. Henry ran around, heading them up the hill. As he did, he could see parties of the island men running, crouched over, down toward the shore. They scattered laterally along a dune at the back of the beach, hiding behind the bushes that grew on top.

Henry looked around. The people in the village all seemed to have left. He dashed over into a small grove of trees a few yards away from the village and knelt down behind the biggest trunk. There were two more volleys of cannon balls into the village and then the three boats crunched onto the sand. The pirates jumped out into the water, waded to shore and pulled the boats up on the beach. Then they moved toward the village in a small mob, their weapons ready.

Suddenly rifles cracked from behind the bushes and a third of the pirates went down. The others yelling, firing wildly, charged at the bushes where the shooters were reloading. As they got near, the other half of the riflemen fired and another third of the pirates went down.

The rest dropped to the sand; those who could fired on the bushes. One of the pirates jumped up waving a saber, yelling for the rest to follow. He ran two steps and was cut down by several bullets. The rest of the pirates were silent. Sporadic rifle fire from the bushes was hitting them. Suddenly, those who were able got up and scurried back to the boats, losing a few more men on the way. Amid a constant trickle of bullets, they launched one of the boats and rowed it back out to the ship.

Firing from behind the sand dune, the settlers finished off the wounded pirates, shooting them in the head as they lay squirming on the sand. Henry could hear angry voices yelling threats from the ship. The ship fired three volleys of grapeshot into the village and the dune, but everyone was under cover and Henry could see no injuries. Finally the ship pulled up its anchors and sailed away.

"The people on Comet Island have made enormous progress in the last few years," said Henry, swirling his wine in the cup. "But it's obvious that we can't go on the way we have. Half the island has told me so in the month since the pirate raid."

Big Joe put his empty cup down on the table and stretched his arms up, extending his fingers to nearly touch a rafter. "That was a great dinner, Henry. Thank you very much. If you feel bothered, you ought to see the way they climb on me. Mostly they want more protection. But also, some of the farmers are complaining about having to leave their work and bring their rifles in.

"Seriously, I can't go on trying to raise an army on the spur of the moment every time a ship comes into the harbor. First, we need a few cannon up on that hill. But I suppose if we get those, the next ship will land somewhere else, and we'll have to be organized to cope with that, too."

Henry glanced around the room. Nora sat in the corner nursing the baby.

"It isn't fair, either," continued Big Joe. "The men who show up when we call for help take all the risks. If they get hurt, it's their tough luck. On top of that they lose a good part of a day's work every time they come in. Some of the men who came here early with you and Seymour just sit back and let the rest of us pull their chestnuts out of the fire. I don't mean the two of you, but you know it's true of some of the others.

"I can tell you it doesn't sit too well with the ones like me who came later and had to work for somebody to get a start. We had to save our money to buy a little piece of land from somebody who came here a few months earlier and got it for nothing. Some of us get a little irritated when we risk our lives to protect what we've built and see that some of you who own a lot more are too busy to come."

Henry said, "Yes, I know. Most of us original settlers were marooned for being uncooperative, and I suppose we haven't changed much. We haven't done anything to even out the burdens on the people here and it is certainly unfair to some of them. But at the same time, we can't afford not to stick together."

Hermann had been nodding his head. "The villagers were pretty useless in fighting pirates, but they know most of the booty is in the village and they want to do their share. They would give a good account of themselves if you organized and trained them, Joe."

"Now that we're getting prosperous we're going to have to defend ourselves," said Seymour. "But, I'd like to bring up some other problems that also need action. We've got all these kids running around. I've got two of the native kids in my house, just as you have, Henry, and mine see yours at school every day. But I'll bet half the kids don't go to school at all. Some of the men who own the most land were quick to grab a wife, but are too stingy to pay for her kids' education. There has been a lot of vandalism this last year and most of it is caused by those kids who are too young for jobs, don't go to school, and are not being controlled by their fathers."

"Absolutely," said Hermann. "They hang around the village and get into trouble. Some of them have never learned English and wouldn't be much use to those of us who hire people. Others who could be working don't seem interested. The island is going to have a big problem unless we teach those kids some skills and some sense of responsibility."

"On top of that, some of the transportation corridors are getting full of holes and ruts," said Seymour. "Just beyond my house a wash is developing; two carts have already turned over in it. For some reason, people seem to think that I should be responsible for it. I don't actually use that part of the road and I refuse to answer for it, although I do go out and do some repair work on it now and then. Somehow, we've all got to get together and fix up the roads so that everyone can use them."

"Another thing," said Hermann. "I've been noticing more and more disputes in the village. Some of the people will no longer agree to use an arbitrator, and in the cases the arbitrators do get they are throwing up their hands because the people haven't agreed on the basis for making the decision. So some people are beginning to break the rules and grab things. They say it's the only way they can get what they're entitled to. It's been leading to fights, even among people you'd expect to know better."

"You don't know the half of it," Big Joe said. "People come to me every day asking for help in those fights. I have no doubt that we're going to have to break down and put in some sort of a government." Big Joe pounded the table for emphasis. Henry winced and looked to see if anything had cracked.

Henry looked over at Nora, who sat watching. The baby was back in the crib. "Nora, could we have some more of that wine, please?" Nora got up to oblige and Henry continued. "One of the men showed me a copy of the constitution they have in America. It seemed to have some interesting ideas and I borrowed it so we could look it over tonight." He unfolded a large printed sheet of paper and laid it on the table. They all leaned forward to look at it.

After they had spent an hour going over the document, Seymour summed up the comments. "This constitution was originally written for the problem they had in coordinating a dozen sovereign states. It's not entirely applicable to our problem of setting up a grass-roots government in a local area. But some of it seems usable and we all agree that there should be a written constitution so that things don't get out of hand once a government has been created."

The discussion continued late into the night and resulted in the start of a draft constitution for Comet Island. All four men agreed that the first thing was to have a legislature. The option of dissolving the social contract when some big problem came along had not been exercised, but everyone worried that it might sometime. The islanders didn't have the time or inclination to spend their days at the meeting meadow fine-tuning the rules. The rules had been getting more complicated anyway and the population was too big now to expect to settle everything in a meeting one day a year. The group agreed that the people would have to elect representatives who could spend the necessary time to develop good laws.

It was evident that the key concession everyone had to make was to agree in advance to obey whatever laws their representatives passed. Some of the islanders were very independent and weren't going to accept this easily, but they finally put it in because they were unable to come up with a practical alternative. Henry was very emphatic that the constitution should limit the scope of the laws that could be passed. The rest agreed, and with this as the key, they buckled down to make a list of the areas in which the legislature could act.

The most urgent need appeared to be an army of some sort to defend the island. They agreed that this was a necessary field for legislative action, but they could not agree to conscription, which Big Joe wanted. A few of the islanders, like Henry, had been shanghaied and were rabidly opposed to forcing anybody into military service. The alternative was to ask for volunteers and pay them, which would require a system of taxation. The idea of paying taxes was repugnant, but Henry argued that they couldn't avoid it and pointed out they would have to pay for the army's supplies and weapons in any case. This led to a discussion of ways to raise money. They reluctantly agreed that there had to be taxes, but couldn't agree on exactly what kind of taxes should be paid. They left the subject by concluding that it was another good area for the legislature.

In addition to raising an army, the group agreed that they needed a road department and schools to take care of the urgent problems in those areas. These three features were all executive operations. So they combined these into an executive branch, to be the responsibility of an official whom the citizens would elect. They were all conscious of the fact that they were sketching a plan for a sovereign state, and it seemed appropriate that this executive should be considered the leader of their state.

When they got to the question of enforcing the laws, they decided to have a police force and a court. They put the two functions together in a justice branch. This system would both enforce the laws and settle disputes between private individuals.

It was near morning when the group broke up. The boys were asleep in the loft and Nora was on the bed next to the baby. The men looked around and lowered their voices, pleased with themselves. The system appeared to be a practical one, although it was apparent that they would have to go back over the provisions and take a lot more care in the wording. The developers of Comet Island's constitution recognized that they faced a major job in getting input from others on the island, letting everyone know about the constitution, and persuading the populace to adopt it.

During the next three months they held meetings with many groups to go over the document, and in many cases they made changes in response to objections and suggestions. By the end of that series of meetings, they felt they had a finished version ready to be offered to the Comet Islanders for acceptance. A fifth of the population had been involved in shaping the document. Men who were familiar with it set up meetings around the island to make everyone aware of each part of the proposed constitution.

Finally, the group of four called for meetings in which the island inhabitants were asked to sign the document, agreeing to be bound by its provisions. They managed to get nearly everyone's signature or mark. This was followed by a general meeting in the meadow where the social contract was usually signed. The citizens of the new state voted on twenty men to act as representatives in a single-house legislature and on the official to run the executive branch. Henry was elected president by acclamation.

Over the next year, the Comet Island government set up a paid militia, appointed policemen and judges, set up a department to improve the roads, and started several public schools, all based on laws passed by the legislature. It also created a system of taxation and appointed people to make the assessments and handle the collections.

For the next several years, Big Joe made a point of turning out some of the militia whenever there was a foreign ship in port. Word of this, along with the fate of the pirates, evidently spread and there were no further attempts to invade the island. Comet Island lived in peace, commerce and industry grew, the population increased, and the members of the island society enjoyed prosperity.

10

The Hybrid Free Society

BASIC OBSERVATIONS

The free society on Comet Island had worked well for several years. Life was simple: the island was predominantly rural, the population density low, and everyone knew everyone else.

But the standard of living had increased, the villages had grown and developed urban characteristics, more people had arrived, and it had become common to meet strangers in the village. Life had become more complicated.

The free-society methods for handling societal problems began to seem inadequate. The islanders were immigrants who were used to living under the authority of governments. While most of them would not have wanted to live again under the same government, they did want to see some of the benefits of a government.

Neither Comet Island nor Ajax Island, in those early days, had a government in the usual sense. In the case of Comet Island, there was no overall societal entity that could act on behalf of the whole population, as a government does. In the case of Ajax Island there was, between the different parts of the society, nothing that corresponded to the distinction between the government and the governed. All the members were equally part of the same active entity.

The constitution on Comet Island established a functioning government by introducing a limited number of status-society rules chosen so that most of the free-society features were largely preserved and interference with the everyday free-society life of most islanders was largely avoided.

It seems appropriate to call this type of society a *hybrid free society,* since its underlying structure is still that of the free society.

Recall that the difference between the pure primary free society and pure primary status society does not imply that societal structures with full or partial status-society rules are absent from a primary free society. Inevitably, status societies of some sort will exist in any prosperous society. But in a primary free society these structures will be secondary status societies—voluntary associations of people in families, businesses, religious congregations, recreational groups, and so forth. The primary status society, in contrast, is one all-encompassing, involuntary status society with no room for secondary societies of any sort.

The members of either a free society or hybrid free society manage their own individual destinies by taking actions that are within their individual spheres of choice. This is the essence of their daily lives. A government that lets them do this, that does not unduly interfere with or diminish the scope of their spheres of choice but increases the value of those spheres, is a good government. The desired government in this kind of society is one that largely works behind the scenes. The desired government is one that is not often encountered by law-abiding, adult members of society who are minding their own business.

An important ethical principle of the free society is that rules should apply in the same way to everyone. There is no appropriate way, in such a society, to design negative rules that apply differently to members on the basis of status without some kind of positive official action on somebody's part to define and establish that status. Perhaps the most appealing example of such a rule would be to say that, as an exception to the rule against stealing, it is all right to steal food if you are starving. But there is no provision for certifying an individual as starving or notifying everyone else who is making decisions that this individual has a unique status. And beyond that, how does the rule define whom the starving person may steal from? Certainly not another starving person. If a starving person steals bread, then is the person to steal from this baker or that? If we knew something of the circumstances, our good judgment would make us very reluctant to punish a starving individual who stole a loaf of bread, but it is not easy to write a rule that permits this where positive judgments are not provided in the rules and, as always, there are various possible hard-to-predict abuses.

This same ethical principle is observed in the hybrid free society, except in rare cases, such as the assessment of property taxes. In that case it is necessary to create a governmental department that acts to classify property and assigns status to the owners.

The internal operations of a hybrid free-society government are conducted along status-society lines, but in many respects this is like the situation in a secondary status society, such as a business. The government employees are volunteers who have accepted their jobs in return for compensation. They owe the government the same kind of nonpersonal-motivation actions that they would if they worked for any status society. Of course the objectives of the government should be chosen in accordance with the societal standard, as they would be in a primary status society.

In a hybrid free society the rules are written so that the government can function in a way that does not conflict with the free-society culture. For one thing, the government avoids impinging on the ordinary citizens' spheres of choice by conducting its operations on its own land and in its own buildings, to the extent reasonable, out of contact with the rest of society. Also, to the extent it functions in public view, the government follows the same negative rules that all the individual members and secondary status societies do. If private vehicles have to stop at a traffic sign, then the government vehicle does, too. If others pay taxes, then government employees do, too. Everyday casual contact with a government that acts on these principles should not be much different from contact with a secondary society, such as a business.

Another important free-society principle is that the rule benefits should be "public goods," benefits that apply to everyone in a general way. While the benefits apply to everyone, the good each member derives from such benefits is not the same. This is something that often causes arguments in the drafting of rules. However, members are free to modify their positions to get more good from a rule if it is important enough to them— a normal aspect of the free society that is carried over into the hybrid free society.

Thus, particularly appropriate to the hybrid free society are those status-society rules and features that also confer a public good—for example, the defense force to protect the state from invasion. The existence of a defense force, even though it is a positive rule feature, avoids some major problems associated with fitting a status-society rule into a hybrid free society because it provides the same type of general benefit distribution as the negative rules.

An alternative hybrid free-society approach used to avoid undue conflict with the underlying negative rules when adding a positive rule that distributes a direct individual benefit, is the uniform benefit, that is, a benefit of equal magnitude to each member of the society. Such benefits will still produce more good for some members than others, but the fact that the benefits are equal keeps members from being concerned that others are getting more favorable treatment.

If the needs and capabilities of the members of society are known or can be measured with reasonable accuracy, then a differential benefit or detriment that is related in an appropriate way to these factors can be an acceptable arrangement, not for a hybrid free society, but for the welfare society that is derived from it. This approach incorporates more status-society principles but is relatively acceptable to free-society people. Unfortunately, even welfare societies do not begin to have adequate facilities, such as one should expect in a well-run status society, for gathering such information or administering such benefits.

Welfare and other further-evolved forms of the free society tend to base some of their benefit distributions on statistical correlations concerning their members: for example, assuming that the members of some group deserve help getting into college because, statistically, fewer of them get in. This type of reasoning may be the product of motivation unrelated to the best interests of the whole membership of society. However, to the extent it is directed to the ethical standard it is a very approximate and unreliable tool. The fact that members in free societies are free to make their own choices leads to substantial interference with the proper working of statistically based distribution programs. This kind of benefit or detriment is undesirable in a hybrid free society and is very hard to justify in a welfare state. Its best use would likely be in areas such as taxation, where detailed numerical data is available so that one could say that two members with the same income should pay the same tax.

In general, the addition of desirable positive rules to a society that has a foundation network of negative rules is much more complicated than the addition of more negative rules. The addition of a negative rule should be justified by showing a net beneficial effect. Adding positive rules involves this same calculation, but it also involves estimating the extent to which operation of the positive rule will be adversely affected by the network of negative rules and the extent to which it will adversely affect the operation of the negative rules. The balancing of benefits and detriments is obviously more complex.

For example, the managers of government departments owe the members their best efforts to do a good job at a low cost. An additional positive requirement that they hire people of a certain status, or that they deal with suppliers with certain political connections cannot help but conflict with the former requirements. It also indirectly injures other potential employees and suppliers. Note that while the rules in a free society do not give members the right to complain of the indirect consequences of other members' actions, this is not the case in the status society, nor does it apply to status-society institutions in a hybrid free-society government.

THE LEGISLATURE

The most prominent governmental institution in a hybrid free society is the legislature, an adaptation of the free-society meeting in which members agree on the social contract and thereby create the society. Agreement on the social contract rules requires unanimity; each member must agree individually on each rule as a prerequisite to membership. The requirement of unanimity makes the social contract appear fragile and impermanent, although, as a practical matter, the ease of reestablishing the social contract could offset much of this.

The hybrid free-society legislature has the same general nature as the social-contract meeting, but to achieve the more vigorous and stable society, the requirement for unanimity must be put aside. This enables the hybrid free society to provide in the rules for the body that makes the rules, for the rules to persist until changed, and for the members to remain in the society unless they move away. In place of unanimity, another criterion has to be substituted and the usual one is the least restrictive one, a simple majority vote. This requires only that more members be for something than against it, which enables the legislature to be powerful and its agenda flexible.

In making membership in the society permanent, the rules require that all of the society's members accept any rules that the legislature may pass in the future. This is a major step beyond the commitment of members in the free society. The town-meeting type of legislature is not well suited to large societies and one would expect instead to have a legislature composed of representatives who can meet for an extended period and discuss in detail any proposed changes in the rules.

In general, the modus operandi of a hybrid free-society legislature should be similar to the social-contract meeting. Both are, in essence, bargaining sessions. The legislators should have a general interest in seeing the society prosper and the people throughout the society achieve their goals, but legislators are likely to be more immediately concerned with taking care of the specific interests of their constituents. Intelligent and enlightened self-interest is capable of producing a good set of rules in such a legislature if the representatives adhere to the relevant principles of the free or status society, as the case may be.

THE EXECUTIVE BRANCH

The most urgent need perceived by the society members on Comet Island was defense against invasion. As noted above, the defense benefit from a military establishment is a public good, which fits well with the pattern of free-society benefits. In addition, the armed forces can easily be operated so that they have little direct effect on the functioning of the society. The army trains on common or government property, which has little impact on how the rest of the people use their private property. When the troops use the roads or other facilities in which they mix with civilians, the military observes the same negative rules that the civilians do. The troops buy and pay for any supplies and accommodations they need.

Staffing of the defense force may be done with volunteers or by the use of conscripts. In peacetime, the decision should reflect the free-society principles in a hybrid free society. The negative-rule system is largely constructed to protect property rights, including the right to one's person. The hybrid free-society government may not forcibly take property any more than an individual member is permitted to do this.

Under emergency conditions, of course, the taking of property may be necessary to preserve the society or to permit it to function in a manner that is reasonably close to the desire of the members. Under these circumstances the right to take property is conferred on the government, provided the owner is compensated. In the case of seizing land, this principle is called eminent domain.

As applied to the conscription of soldiers, compensation should at least be provided for the time taken from their ordinary activities. The value the state should pay the soldier depends on the value of these activities. Thus, some conscripted soldiers should be paid substantially more for their time than others, quite apart from their role in the military organization. Of course, if every member of the society (with no exceptions for age or health, etc.) were conscri ted, such as might happen in a severe emergency, then this might be considered similar to taxation. In that case there is a universally applied detriment and the applicable principles will be discussed later.

Under normal circumstances and in peacetime the use of volunteers would probably be less expensive than the use of properly compensated conscripts because of the usual market situation, namely that the government will only have to pay as much per soldier as it takes to attract the marginal recruit.

The road department is another institution that can fit easily into a state that is fundamentally free society in operation. As in the case of the army, it operates internally like a production subsociety of a primary status society, or, for that matter, like a business (a secondary status society). Its external operations can be run in a fashion that is compatible with the network of free-society rules.

As with the other status-society-derived government departments that are part of the hybrid free society, the road department has an obligation to do the best it can for the society within its area of responsibility. It is common in this field to contract work out to private companies on a lowest-bid-for-performance basis. In this case the result is specified, but not the details of the contractor's actions. For this approach to satisfy the ethical principles requires that the road department be able to specify the results precisely and monitor them adequately.

The benefits of a system of roads constitute a public good, but the system may take years to complete. Thus people who are positioned geographically to get these benefits early in the program have a major advantage. The alternative is to provide the road system as a uniform benefit. This can be done by giving everyone an equal chance in a lottery, that is to say, picking by chance the order in which the roads are built. Obviously, this objective may have to be balanced against the economic benefits of building the roads in some order that optimizes production efficiency.

The education department is affected by the same principles as the road department. In this case, the department's direct beneficiary is a status group, the young. It goes against free-society principles to confer a benefit selectively on a status group, but all are young for at least part of their lives and thus the benefit may be viewed as approximately uniform.

Unlike the road department, the education department is probably not as capable of specifying desired results or monitoring them. Nevertheless, it may be desirable, in some cases, to work through contractors. As an alternative to the lowest-bid-to-meet-specifications basis, it may be more efficacious to use a best-efforts relationship with contractors. Unlike the road contracts, the contractor here would no longer be entitled to perform the work independently, but rather should function as an extension of the education department. The contractor thereby takes on the status-society obligations of a government employee.

The army, the road department, and the education department are still parts of the executive function of a government and are derived from the production part of a status society. The ethical principles that apply to the operations inside these departments are fundamentally those that apply in status-society production departments. The employees should use their best efforts to benefit society, and none of their decisions should be affected by their personal motives. The principles require coordination and teamwork on the job. Thus the ethical principles for the behavior of people in the executive departments are quite different from those for the legislators.

At the same time, the ethical principles that the executive departments apply to external relationships must be those appropriate to their position in a network of free-society rules. Their activities should be carried on in ways that do not violate the negative rules, and they should treat every member of the public alike. One of the things that distinguishes the hybrid free society is that the production department functions lend themselves to this.

THE JUDICIAL BRANCH

The police and the judiciary are adaptations of the distribution departments in a primary status society. A judiciary is missing some of the power of the distribution department because its authority to write rules is shared with the legislature. Both the judiciary and the legislature have an appropriate function in establishing rules. The legislature must have an ability to investigate and weigh the many viewpoints that should be considered in formulating a new law. The judiciary must have the ability to narrow the rules to specific cases. However, the judiciary is constrained by its case format to announcing rules as though they had been in force all along, which largely precludes making arrangements for the gradual introduction of new laws. The judiciary is thus inherently less well-equipped to make substantial changes in the rules than the legislature.

On the other hand, it is important in a society that functions largely on free-society premises that substantial changes in the rules be infrequent. The legislature, by virtue of its bargaining nature, can easily stray into making too many rule changes and changes that ignore ethical principles. It is not well-equipped to make complicated logical analyses. In being responsive to their constituents, the legislators are likely to pass new rules that are not well thought out.

The benefits of the hybrid free society depend on having rules that follow ethical principles, which call for restraining the authority of the legislature, and limiting the judiciary to its appropriate sphere of responsibility. Compared to the distribution managers in the status society, the judiciary has a smaller area of authority. In part, this reflects the fact that free-society members should expect to satisfy their objectives by their own actions and not by what the court will do for them. Instead of making sure people achieve the good, as the distribution managers do, the judiciary and the police department in a hybrid free society largely have the job of correcting and punishing.

TAXES

Along with the benefits that status-society rules and features add to a free society, there will be detriments, notably taxes. As in the case of benefits, a detriment will best fit into the free-society framework if it is general—in effect, a reverse public good. Import duties might serve as an example. However, import duties may cause too much detriment—for instance, diminished trade and competition—to be an efficient way to raise money unless there are other benefits, such as shielding fledgling industries. While the public goods have a generally favorable effect on the society and justify the attitude of the more the better, reverse public goods have an unfavorable effect and should be minimized.

The principal hybrid free-society alternative for raising money is to use taxes that have a uniform impact on the individual members of society. One thing that all members have in equal measure is time, one year per year. Their time itself is perhaps not of much value to the government, but to the extent people devote their time to producing economic goods, the government may find those useful. The government might, thus, logically ask that a member contribute per year the average amount of money that he or she received in a specified number of days, which is to say a specified percentage of his or her income. In like fashion, a specified percentage of one's property might be required as taxes.

Such taxes are compatible with free-society distinctions. Alternatively, one might consider other approaches, such as the progressive income tax, which stems from status-society principles. In the status society, contributions are asked from members on the basis of their capability, taking into account also the amount of detriment caused to their ultimate purposes. Progressive taxes are not desirable in a hybrid free society. The government does not have the apparatus for judging the effect of rules on members' ultimate purposes.

CONCLUSION

The hybrid free society can be a highly desirable and successful form of primary society because the free-society fundamentals confer flexibility. The addition of those status-society features that do not much interfere with free-society features does not significantly reduce the benefits that flow from them. At the same time, the added status-society features confer security and stability and, one would hope, a law-abiding citizenry.

11

Slipping Ideals

Coming into the great Ajax Island dining hall on a sunny afternoon, the group of three men and two women paused to let their eyes adjust to the dim light. They barely saw the rafters high up underneath the pitched roof. It was as though they had come into a huge barn. Looking ahead, they saw regular patterns of light caused by shiny reflections from the spotless floor and table tops. The room had been scrubbed after lunch, the tables aligned precisely in rows, and the chairs arranged neatly around them.

In a corner at the far end of the room, a flickering glow from the fireplace made a halo around the semicircle of chairs that faced it. The middle chair had a higher back than the rest, and as the group walked toward it, they saw Andrew's mane of white hair sticking up over the top. Three decades had passed, and Andrew's ninetieth birthday had been celebrated in the dining hall a few weeks before. He had stopped participating in the management some years ago and spent much of his day sitting in front of the fire. But he was alert, his opinions were valued above all others, and he was still the society's inspiration.

The men and women in the approaching group were all in their early thirties. They were the top managers of their generation, the first that had grown up completely on Ajax Island without the memory of previous ways of life in other communities. Quietly, they surrounded Andrew as Albert, their spokesperson, said, "Sir?"

Andrew looked up. "None of that now! I'm still spry enough to be a participant. Humph, I resent being addressed as though I were some kind of icon." He frowned at them, and then smiled fondly. "Go ahead, sit down. Looks like the future leaders of the society are paying me a visit."

As the five took their seats, Albert spoke again, "We came to ask your thoughts on a problem that worries us." He paused. "The most pressing symptom of the problem is disruption of the discussion sessions by the young people. One week they insist on talking all the time; the next they won't even answer a civil question; and the week after that they giggle. . . ."

Andrew, nodding his head, interrupted. "The teenagers again? You have to be patient and not take them too seriously. They grow out of it."

Althea, one of the women in the group, spoke up. "It's not that easy and the problem goes beyond the teenagers. These days, the people in their twenties are impatient and unwilling to pursue ideas in depth. Some of our own generation get obsessed with exotic theories that anybody should be able to see are wild and unrealistic. The middle-aged people act bored and a lot of the older people say they are indisposed and miss the sessions altogether. We have continued the tradition of including a mixture of ages in each discussion group, but it doesn't seem to be providing members with a broad perspective anymore. People just get irritated at viewpoints that are too different from their own."

Andrew grinned, his eyes twinkled, and his face took on a quizzical expression. "All right, all right, let's get to the point."

Albert leaned forward. "This group is profoundly grateful to you for giving us the responsibility for the discussion sessions. We have been trying our best—everything we could think of—to keep the meetings up to the standard you set. But regardless of what we do in the meetings, we just keep getting a poorer and poorer response."

Andrew looked at the fire. His chin dropped a little and he shook his head slowly.

Albert resumed. "At first we thought we had a whole group of problems because the symptoms were different from one person to the next. Then we noticed the symptoms depended on the age of the member, so we have tried to modify the program at one time or another to appeal to each of the age groups. But it hasn't worked. We finally concluded that it's all one problem: our comrades are just no longer benefiting from studying philosophy for as many hours a week as they used to." He paused and then spoke slowly. "We have reluctantly concluded that the philosophy discussions are not going to do as much for the Society as they did when you ran them."

"So you think we ought to cut down on the number of philosophy discussions?" said Andrew patiently. "Don't think this hasn't come up before. The problem we always face is figuring out what to do with the time. I can remember listening to lengthy discussions of putting our members back to work building infrastructure or making things to sell to the rest of the world so we could buy luxuries. Bu we always arrived at the same question: Would those programs bring us closer to our fundamental goal?"

No one replied to this, so Andrew went on. "We get all the nutritious food we need. We exercise and keep our weight at reasonable levels. We take care of medical problems promptly. Our population growth rate is modest, so we don't need any general expansion of the facilities. We've developed as much of the island as we can use. I don't think any of you would want to cut down any more of the jungle and needlessly threaten the life of our animal neighbors. We certainly wouldn't want to change the island in some way our descendants would regret." Andrew looked around. The members of the group squirmed a little in their chairs. None of them spoke for a moment.

"I understand the problems," said Albert, finally. "We didn't have more infrastructure or luxuries in mind. But at the same time, we think the society should consider making a significant modification to the system in some direction. Is it possible that by now the members of our society are just inherently less able to get as much good from philosophy as the group that came over on the ship?"

Andrew sat a minute in thought. In the silence the group listened to the crackle of the fire and watched while it flared up for a moment and then settled back. "I suppose that could be the case," said Andrew. "It's been thirty years. People change. Children are only somewhat like their parents. Not everybody is constituted so that philosophy will be the answer to reaching their fundamental goals."

There was another pause. Andrew looked around the circle, and spoke mildly. "What specific changes did you have in mind?"

"After wrestling with this problem for months," Albert said, "we have unanimously arrived at the proposal that we substitute a music program for half of the philosophy discussion program. Specifically, we would build an orchestra and chorus. Some of the members in our parents' generation have musical experience and could be used as leaders.

"I should mention that some of the people have suggested that we offer choices. We felt strongly that to offer choices would upset the whole mechanism we use to manage the society. It would authorize people to spend time thinking selfishly about what they want and then make selfish choices. We are committed to continuing the action to avoid personal motives completely since that has been so successful here. Changing the nature of the program in this direction, we think, will bring people closer to their fundamental goals, and it doesn't violate any of our principles."

"We've been worrying," explained Althea, "about the possibility that the music program would do more good for some members than others. It is clear that the philosophy program does everybody some good and, following your lead, we always estimate that it is substantially the same amount of good per hour for everyone, which simplifies our benefit calculations. We think the music program will come close to matching that effect and can be managed on the same basis. To the extent this is not precisely correct, we think it likely that things will even out because the members who get less good from the music program will be those who get more good from the philosophical discussions."

Andrew leaned back in his chair, lost in thought. It was clear to him that the young managers did not grasp the fundamentals of the society, did not adequately understand how it was supposed to work. He felt momentarily sick. These bright young people, whom he loved, thought that the society, as he had set it up originally, was intended to go on running the same way forever.

He remembered all the difficulties he had organizing the society, recruiting the members, and raising the money; then the multitude of problems he had to overcome in getting the society settled on Ajax Island, and operating in the manner he had planned.

Andrew knew from the beginning the weakness in his theory, the difficulty in pinning down each individual's fundamental goal. What others saw as an objection, he viewed as an opportunity. As soon as all the other nagging but urgent little problems had been settled, he had intended to embark on a grand search for a deeper understanding of fundamental goals and for better techniques to characterize the fundamental goal in each individual.

The years had slipped away. During the last few, he had relaxed in the glow of a job well done, a society where everyone was happy, a land where reason ruled and all was as it should be. He had grown old sitting by the fire basking in the adulation of the young people of whom he was so proud.

The choice of philosophy discussions had been made very early. He was confident that there were others like himself who could get more good from philosophy than anything else. He had found such people, and that had enabled him to build a fine, workable society. But he had never meant to stop there. Of course, there were going to be people who needed something else in life. The key was for the managers to refine their techniques for learning the fundamental goals and for determining what would be good for the various types.

A pang of fear seized Andrew. The time was short. Unless the society developed substantially better diagnostic techniques quickly, it would begin to act on some other basis—individual wants or drives, most likely—and probably never get back to the original vision.

Andrew sat up and looked at Albert. "On what basis did you choose music?"

"We talked to everyone in the last few years to find out what they were interested in. Music was the subject that came closest to having universal appeal," Albert said, smiling.

"Have you made any attempt to relate music to the fundamental goals of your members?"

Albert looked perplexed. "Not exactly. Music seems to be highly regarded by the philosophers. I guess we felt that practical considerations took precedence. Orienting the program toward the members' fundamental goals is a nice theory, but I don't think that any of us know how to use it in a practical situation of this complexity."

"I'm sorry you take that position," said Andrew. "But I can understand why you say it and I blame myself. I really think that before we embark on a new program, we ought, as a society, to make a strong, creative effort to push our knowledge of fundamental goals ahead to the point where it will be useful in solving the problem you have described. With your permission, I would like to speak about this to the whole society at the session tomorrow."

Andrew took charge of the discussion sessions again and galvanized everyone into action. There was an explosion of ideas. People were divided into teams that investigated various aspects of the problem of determining fundamental goals. There was an eagerness to work long hours; it reminded the older members of the first few months on the island. All the members shared a feeling of getting back on the track.

Andrew put in long days directing, moderating, explaining. Everyone was amazed at his energy and the vigor with which he conducted the program. But then one day, about five weeks later, Andrew worked especially late. The next morning he awoke unable to speak or rise from his bed. The doctors clustered anxiously around him. The whole society waited nervously. He lived only three more days.

The society buried Andrew with great ceremony and many speeches. The whole society lapsed into a period of intense mourning, eschewing the philosophy programs and many of the other production programs. This went on for nearly two months.

Finally, the society came out of its sorrow and started back into the regular discussion sessions. The managers attempted to pick up the program of discovery of fundamental goals that Andrew had been leading. What had seemed so clear before was now not very meaningful. After a few months of trying, the leaders reverted to the old program and the discussions of philosophy. As the months wore on, the various symptoms of boredom began to reappear. Albert and the group became concerned and looked again at various possibilities.

Ultimately, the group of young managers brought up the plan they had reviewed with Andrew. After several presentations and a thorough discussion, it was approved by the top management. The society cut the time for philosophy discussions in half and used the other half for the music program. The managers ordered instruments and sheet music sent from Europe, using money the society had built up from exports. The managers were pleased to find that there was a sizable pool of musical talent. But there were other members with less talent and the managers constructed a varied program of musical activities that provided even the least-endowed members a full measure of participation.

The music program was clearly a popular success; nearly everybody experienced some good from its benefits, and morale shot up. The philosophy discussions also benefited from the new attitudes shown by the members. The orchestra played for the chorus and the chorus sang for the orchestra. Occasionally they performed jointly for everyone's benefit.

The only sour note in this societal satisfaction came from some of the distribution managers. They had been juggling a complex system, one in which they already made use of oversimplifications, such as the assumption that everyone made the same progress toward his or her fundamental goal by participating in the philosophy discussions for the same amount of time. The distribution managers had been discussing a system to measure the actual amount of good the individual member achieved, but the proposed system was a long way from being ready for use.

With the addition of the music program, the problem became much more complicated. It seemed obvious that some of the members were getting more out of the music program than the philosophy program and vice versa. This motivated the managers to try harder to measure the good that resulted. At the same time, they could see that such knowledge would ultimately drive them to specify that one individual have more of one program, another more of the other program. The problems this would present to the production managers might well be beyond their capabilities.

What emerged from this assessment of the two programs was the assumption that everyone got the same amount of good from an hour in either program. The managers felt that they were being forced to settle for less precise approximations in their calculations of good. This led them to feel that it would be fruitless to fine-tune the job assignments as much as they had been. The distribution managers told themselves that the end results had improved overall, but obviously the managers had less control of these results.

Ajax Island had been settled in a period when most of the people in the world, including Europe, spent their time cultivating the land and producing the necessities of life under crude living conditions. Initially, the New Socratic Society clearly enjoyed a higher average standard of living than most other sovereign states. With disciplined and enlightened teamwork on an island that had an excellent climate and adequate natural resources, the society produced the necessities of life and still had time left over for the intellectual pursuits that were at the heart of Andrew's prescription for a good life. Unlike the inhabitants of the islands to the south, the members of the society on Ajax Island did not waste time in idle gossip and excessive recreational pursuits, but spent these hours in more cerebral activities, making progress toward their fundamental goals.

But things were changing in the world. Technology was advancing. The Industrial Revolution was turning out products that appealed to everyone and were attractively priced so that they could be distributed widely. Some of the luxuries that had been available only to the upper classes began to show up among the common people. Knowledge of such things, of the possibilities of various alternatives to their way of life, came to Ajax Island. Dissatisfaction with various aspects of their lives began to build up in the members of that society.

Another decade passed. The top managers retired and Albert moved into the position of leader of the society. The character of the comrades continued to evolve. Some were neither verbal nor musical. Typically they wanted to spend time working with their hands, and several had an overwhelming impulse to paint or sculpt. In response, the discussion programs were gradually diversified to include workshops on a wide variety of subjects in the humanities and the arts.

With the addition of more subjects, the managers gave up the practice of having everyone in the society in the same discussion meeting at once. Instead, they developed a discussion program in which different people went to different discussions at different times, depending on their requirements. The managers continued to interview members at regular intervals, but as a practical matter, it was no longer feasible for the managers to view themselves as deriving the daily activity for a member from his fundamental goal. The managers assigned people to the activities they thought intuitively would do them the most good and were strongly influenced by the members' expressions of what they wanted to do.

Philosophy, humanities, and the arts were all changing in the world outside and the discussions were often lively. However, science and technology were changing even more. The managers, influenced by Andrew's ideas, remained convinced that science was a relatively sterile form of intellectual activity. Members asked for programs in this area, but the management was slow to respond.

People continued to change. Some of the next generation were not interested in discussions at all. They wanted to do different things. They demanded sports, gardening, more handicrafts, and the like. The managers were disappointed, but they gave in and instituted activities in these areas also.

Despite the training to act without personal motives and to think always of the good of the whole society, some of the members insisted they be assigned specific activities merely because they enjoyed doing them. These members not only argued with managers about what they should do during the program periods, but demanded the option to choose their activity according to what attracted them most on a particular day. They demanded the right to be spontaneous.

This actually did not represent much change in the way things were working. The practice of appraising fundamental goals and designing an activity program that produced the most good had long since become a ritual, observed only briefly in form and not in substance. The managers did not want to give up this ritual, but the members appealed to the society's top management and it eventually acquiesced to the members' demands. This had the consequence of reducing the distribution managers' role in activities to that of mere advisors.

Although, at the time, it seemed merely a step in the process of liberalization, the Rubicon was crossed when members were permitted to select their own day-to-day activities. For the first time, the individual member was officially put in the position of being asked to make a choice on a selfish basis. Almost unnoticed was the fact that this seemed to come quite naturally to most of them, despite the decades of training they had received in avoiding personally motivated thinking.

Even though the distribution managers had lost the battle, they did not give up the cause. When they saw some of the members avoiding intellectual activities, the managers scolded them and instituted compulsory attendance at certain fundamental lectures. Unfortunately, as with most compulsory activities, this alienated members and turned them against all intellectual activities.

The society grew slowly and occupied eight villages in different parts of the island. It was still a close-knit community and everything was done in groups led by the managers. All the members continued to live in dormitories and to eat in communal dining halls. Materialistic things were considered to be of little importance.

Then a problem arose with the members making handicrafts. Their output—pieces of jewelry, knick-knacks, small pieces of furniture—had no real permanent place in the society. The managers had always decreed that such objects should be exported or destroyed after the maker had experienced the piece for a while. Otherwise, they feared, the handicrafts would come to clutter up the villages.

Keeping a few sentimental decorations around each comrade's sleeping place had already been recognized as potentially good. The society usually ordered a member to keep a few such things when it felt that they would have that effect. But the handicrafters wanted the right to keep things they had made, even when the managers wanted them exported or destroyed.

The managers said no and pointed out that this meant introducing private property rights. The issue was argued at length in the discussion sessions. It became clear that most of the members wanted a few things of their own. The top managers finally gave in and permitted members to designate a limited number of items that they could thereafter look upon as their own.

A few years later, currency was introduced with the practice of selling certain types of items in stores. This did not have the effect it does in a market economy, since the distribution managers continued to specify how much of each item was to be produced, a system that had worked smoothly when the managers controlled distribution on an individual basis. When things were sold in the store, however, some of the items specified by the distribution managers sold out quickly and others languished on the shelves. In a general way the managers took this into account and increased the production request on the items that the customers preferred. However, they considered some of the popular items to be trivial. The distribution managers could not forget their underlying responsibility to see that good was maximized. Thus they continued to order items they thought the members ought to have and only secondarily the ones that sold out first.

On the surface, the New Socratic Society continued to function smoothly. Underneath, however, there were many stresses. Many of the members wanted still more freedom. However, on the production side everyone continued to work as a team and the volume of output was quite satisfactory.

12

The Hybrid Status Society

EVOLUTION OF THE HYBRID STATUS SOCIETY ON AJAX ISLAND

There are status societies, such as Eskimo families, using primitive technology in environments so severe that even survival can be considered a good outcome. In such circumstances, the members may have an overriding common interest in the necessities: staying alive, getting enough to eat, having something to wear, shelter, sex, and taking care of the young. A relationship that is largely status society may be the most efficient way to satisfy these needs.

However, in primitive societies that are even modestly more prosperous, individuals have access to benefits beyond necessities: imported items, for example. In such societies the team relationship is ordinarily loosened enough to allow individuals to pursue their own disparate objectives. Although the society on Ajax Island was reasonably prosperous, the original society operation was greatly simplified because the members did share an overriding interest, their interest in philosophy. Such a condition was unlikely to continue in a primary society, and when it faded, adjustments were made.

The course that the adjustment took on Ajax Island was not necessarily typical. There might, instead, have been a violent upheaval, a drifting away of the population to more interesting places, a new set of rules and managers, or some other development. As it happened, the continuous adjustments that took place on Ajax Island progressed smoothly along a path in which more and more free-society features were introduced. Regardless of how they crept into the rules, these adjustments suggest some of the elements that may differ between a status society and a hybrid status society.

The first step on Ajax Island was to double the number of discussion program subjects, from one to two. This did not change the basic nature of the program, but it complicated the calculation of maximum good, a calculation that is a key factor in the management of a status society. Thus the advantages that diversification brought were offset to some degree by the disadvantages of less precise management.

Later, additional subjects were added to the program. Quite likely these subjects added value, but in a pure status society they would have been accompanied by a system for prescribing individual curricula specifically tailored for the ultimate purpose of each member. Quantification of this type would have been so difficult as to be impossible for the managers on Ajax Island. Poor though the assumption was, they wound up assuming that an hour spent by A on X was equivalent to an hour spent by B on Y. So again, the optimization techniques deteriorated.

The managers already felt somewhat inadequate in the task of discerning good based on the members' ultimate purposes. It is not unlikely that this would have been true for other standards of good, too. In addition, the problems of relative evaluation between amounts of good for different members were exacerbated. In judging the results of the programs, the managers began to rely on the members' opinions. The members' degree of appreciation became the new *de facto* standard of good. As a practical matter, to get the advantages of this much diversification, the ideal of using ultimate purpose, or some other objective standard of good, was abandoned.

The new standard, member's preference, was only applied to assigning places in the discussion groups. The original standard of ultimate purpose was still the official criterion and used by the managers for all the other decisions. This left the system suffering from lack of consistency.

The members knew that the managers were basing their discussion-group decisions on members' preferences, something members knew more about than managers. It does not take long, in such a situation, for the members to conclude that they should do their own choosing. This leads to demands for new products based on the desires of those making the demands. It also leads to the demand that a member be allowed to make up an individual schedule in accordance with personal preferences.

The offering of many consumption choices by a hybrid status society is not consistent with the status-society commitment to manage members' lives so that they achieve optimum good, measured by an objective standard.

Abandoning the objective standard puts the responsibility for consumption choices on the individual member, as is done in the free society. However, in the free society this is the foundation; other rules are oriented toward facilitating these choices. In the hybrid status society, the other rules are largely oriented toward supporting the team effort to maximize the good. Allowing people to do what they wanted removed the managers' authority over the discussion group assignments on Ajax Island, but the managers were still charged with many other tasks. They still set the production requirements; they still distributed the necessities; and they still tried to balance the time a member spent on production and consumption.

The objective of the distribution manager had been to optimize good for the entire population. Now there existed an area in which the managers were barred from doing this. It was not clear that the managers' general objective had been changed. The managers still had to decide how to fit into their calculations the effects of the discussion groups on individuals. Should they have ignored these effects and optimized the remaining part of the lives of the individuals? Or should they have tried to optimize a member's entire program, including the member's choices?

The managers felt that the exclusions from their authority were misguided. They felt they knew better than the members what the latter should be doing, and were sad to see members make wrong choices. The managers felt, as had Andrew, that intellectual activities were by far the best way to achieve the good. On the other hand, members seemed to want to spend a lot of their free time on sports, gossip, and idleness. In this kind of situation, the managers strove to counteract what they perceived as the wrong impulses of the members. One approach they took was to narrow the field of choice, offering only the activities they thought were good for the members.

The freedoms given to the members of the New Socratic Society were prized, but the members did not see it as enough. In fact, it was not enough to produce the kinds of benefits that free-society members enjoy. The inability to choose their production activities, along with consumption ones, for example, frustrated many members. The members and the managers continued to be mutually frustrated in their struggle to have the authority to make decisions. Members chafed at their inability to undertake long-range projects because the managers continued to make changes in the rules. But the managers insisted on adjusting the rules from time to time to optimize societal results as they saw them.

The inclusion of private-property rights and obligations in the hybrid status society blocks off another area from the exercise of status-society mechanisms. On Ajax Island a compromise was reached between the managers and the members in which the latter could own various consumer items without interference by the managers, but they were not allowed to own items that had productive capacity, such as printing presses.

An advantage of the institution of private property is that it provides something close to free-society benefits in certain realms, provided it is treated with respect by the managers. A disadvantage is that it provides an area in which selfish motives appear to produce more good for members than they get in functions in which they must act without personal motives. This interferes with status-society discipline and reduces the members' ability to exclude personal motives from those decisions that require such exclusion.

Money and markets were also included in the hybrid status society on Ajax Island. Money facilitated the transactions between members that would have been going on *sub rosa* anyway and brought some of the benefits of a free market to hybrid status-society members. It did not bring the major benefit of a precise and rational method of regulating production. The production managers were still scheduling production according to a schedule of requirements from the distribution managers.

The distribution managers, since they had to specify production targets for items not distributed through markets anyway, also did the official interpretation of what the market was saying. The distribution managers estimated the amounts of various benefits they thought would be sold, and provided this information to the manufacturing plants as production targets. As might be expected, the managers adjusted their estimates of demand by incorporating their ideas of what it would be good for the members to buy. They also influenced purchases by setting low prices on items they thought were good for people, and higher prices on items that they thought were not.

DESIGNING A HYBRID STATUS SOCIETY

Designing the rules for a hybrid status society brings up much different problems from those encountered in designing rules for a hybrid free society. The status society has a very complicated design because the rules in its institutions are interlocked; each rule affects the others. The primary free society is much simpler because the rules have much less effect on each other and can be evaluated incrementally.

In a sense the primary status society is analogous to a crystalline solid, while the primary free society is more like a liquid. More particularly,

the free society is like a stew with chunks of solid secondary status societies floating around in it. The difference between a free society and a
hybrid free society is mainly that governmental chunks have been added
to the stew.

To carry this analogy a little further, the difference between a status
society and a hybrid status society is the presence of some liquidity in
the latter. Introducing liquidity into a rigid structure is not as easy as
introducing solids into a liquid. Conceivably the whole status-society
network could be made more flexible, but it is difficult to see how. A
more likely way to design a rigid crystalline structure that has some liquidity
is to make holes in the crystal and let them fill with liquid. Be that as
it may, the hybridization of a status society, in the way that it was done
on Ajax Island, involved severing many of the connections that enabled
the status society members to coordinate their work as a team.

The most prominent ethical principle of the status society is that the
choice of actions must not be affected by personal motivations. The hybrid
status society authorizes a whole range of selfish actions by the members.
To the extent that a significant portion of the choices are in the hands
of the members as individuals, the society has divided responsibility. In
part, the society's managers may still exert authority as though the effects
of the actions were borne by the society as an entity, but the individual
members are now making choices on the basis of the effect such actions
have on them. Many of the choices being made by individual members
for their own benefit may have an adverse effect on the society. The hybrid
status society is missing much of the characteristic of undivided responsibility
found in the pure status society.

The hybrid status society has a powerful government that can bring
substantial force to bear on members to make them do as they are told.
Because of this, strong internal pressures can build up in the members.
The leadership can reduce the pressures by giving members a bit more
freedom, and the strength of the organization will permit the leadership
to retain successful control of the society indefinitely.

Unfortunately, the hybrid status society no longer retains most of the
ethical principles of the pure status society, and it doesn't incorporate many
of the free-society ethical principles either. In other words, the hybrid status
society probably can be a stable compromise between status-society and
free-society features, but it no longer has much capacity to achieve the
most good for the overall membership, because it no longer has the tools.
A stable society is reached in the course of abandoning ethical principles.

SPECULATIONS ON DESIGNING RULES

How might this have been done differently? The steps taken on Ajax Island reflect the modifications in a status society forced on the management by a restive population. Note that this kind of modification cannot be like converting a free society to a hybrid free society by adding (status-society) rules on top of the existing network of (free-society) rules. Adding (free-society) rules on top of an existing network of (status-society) rules would create a mess in which rules contradict other rules to a major degree.

The first step in introducing free-society features into a status society should be to remove some of the positive rules. This creates the holes in the crystal. Once the society's managers withdraw from making the decisions in an area, the society can permit members to make the decisions themselves. The first aim is to put decisions concerning the welfare of an individual in the hands of that individual. Examples would be giving members permission to choose their own benefits, speak their own thoughts, and exercise their own preferences.

In a later stage, the aim is to take advantage of the marketplace as a mechanism for motivation, for distribution, and, most of all, as a source of information. The marketplace provides a mechanism that integrates information from many individuals acting on their own initiative for their own purposes. The marketplace works well to the extent that individuals are free to make choices on both sides of the trades, and beyond that are free to make and consume things without other constraints.

Given freedom to do a range of things, the member may choose to do some that cannot be permitted for the same reasons that motivate the rules in a free society. It is only in response to this possibility that negative rules must be introduced to exclude such choices.

Thus the areas to be thrown open for free choice are chosen bearing in mind the areas where freedom is likely to elicit the best from individuals and be least damaging to the continued operation of the underlying network of status-society rules. Then attention should be turned to governance of the remaining part of the society that is to continue in the status-society mode. The design of a status-society set of rules requires an objective and a game plan leading to a coordinated set of activities that will bring the society to the objective. A set of rules must be written to direct the members to take the actions needed to put this plan into effect.

Once the plan for the status-society portion of the projected hybrid status-society rules has been completed, the free-society area is defined in more detail by the areas of expected activity that are left over. Given the fluid nature of free-society activities, it is not necessary to have objectives and a well-defined game plan in the free area. Negative rules may then be written to control the activities in this area for the protection of societal activities and those of the individual members.

Of course, to make a free-society set of features work well requires that certain basic free-society ethical principles be observed. For example, the negative rules should be applied in the same way to everyone. If ignored, the lack of such principles may result in a free area that is too constricted or unprotected from the managers to be of use. It may be necessary to iterate the planning back and forth until both the free-society area and the status-society area have the facilities they need to function efficiently.

A hybrid status society, if properly organized in accordance with status-society ethical principles, is a machine that can be operated to maximize good for its members. It needs to be a much more finely coordinated and balanced organization than a free society. The free-society features can fit into nooks and crannies, although for maximum good, free-society principles, such as not changing the rules, should be observed.

13

A Dictator

During the thirty years of Albert's leadership, the New Socratic Society had been transformed from a disciplined, intellectual community into one that had a much broader range of interests—material, social, and physical as well as intellectual—and one that had substantial areas of individual choice. Decades later it was still on the surface a well-behaved community and one where the inhabitants seemed to be content, although not pleased, with their lot in life.

The society still owned nearly everything, although the members were entitled to have individual possession and use of the items they collected in certain categories, including their apartments, clothing, household and kitchen tools, recreational equipment, art, and so forth. Each member was still assigned a job, worked at it, and was paid for the work. The pay varied with one's status in the society. In their free time, the inhabitants spent their money and engaged in nearly any activity they wanted to, except only that they had to avoid involvement in anti-societal activities as defined by the managers.

The society's managers ran all of the production facilities, stores, and any place that people worked. Working in one's apartment to make money was not countenanced. Even comrades who had jobs as artists and writers worked in properly appointed studios. The apartments and other community buildings were tastefully designed, painted in earth colors, well-maintained, and free of graffiti or vandalism of any sort. The areas were landscaped with trees and bushes, and the overall appearance of both the villages and the countryside was pleasant although somewhat austere.

119

Some of the Ajax Islanders visited Comet Island from time to time and reported that they were shocked at the bright colors, the clutter of signs, the way people walked around briskly and the way they sometimes talked to each other in abrasive, even abusive tones. Nevertheless, it was evident that the people on Comet Island had a standard of living that was, in conventional terms, higher than that of Ajax Island. However, there was a large difference in the degree of affluence, between rich and poor, on Comet Island. In any case, many of the possessions of the affluent Comet Islanders were of little interest to the Ajax Islanders. A great deal of it was trivial. But it was also true that the Comet Islanders had more books, more art objects, more athletic equipment, and more and better food. The people on Comet Island seemed to work harder and have more capital equipment of all sorts.

Comet Island was a mixed-race society, composed of whites, Polynesians, and those of mixed parentage, with the latter being the majority. This didn't seem to matter on Comet Island, but the visitors from Ajax Island, who were mostly of northern European descent, had a mildly adverse reaction.

Both societies continued on their respective paths for several more decades, having little to do with one another. Ajax Island fell steadily behind in terms of standard of living, and some of its members felt that they were in a backwater. The Ajax Islanders agreed, however, that their society was intellectually and culturally superior. But this did not erase the feeling that something was missing. While they were repelled by the chaotic way that Comet Island seemed to run, and scornful of the poor taste shown by many Comet Islanders, they were nonetheless attracted to the vigor of the society there.

Finally, it happened that on the retirement of a current leader, the Central Committee on Ajax Island was able to elevate an exceptionally promising and charismatic man as the new leader of the society. This leader, Arnold, had shown great promise at an early age, had been identified as the future society leader, and pushed to the front of his management group as a young man. He had moved through all aspects of the society, filling at one time or another nearly every job on the island. In the last half-dozen years, he had been given intensive experience in top management, rotating through all the major managerial posts. As a result, he knew not only how to do all the jobs and had ideas for how to do them better, but was well acquainted with all the managers who would now be his subordinates. Despite all this experience, Arnold was in his early forties, the youngest leader in the history of the New Socratic Society.

Arnold immediately gathered a staff of the best young managers and set them to work for three months to develop a comprehensive plan for the future of the society. He spent most of his own time with them on this project, leaving day-to-day activities in the hands of experienced managers in whom he had confidence. Then, with a new seven-year plan in hand, he set out to persuade the whole society to throw its full weight behind the program.

Arnold started by meeting with his predecessor and other senior statesmen of the society. They gave him their enthusiastic blessing. Then he presented the plan to the Central Committee in a series of meetings in which he went over it in minute detail. He insisted that they master the plan and bring up any questions or contrary opinions. Arnold patiently presented the arguments and answers based on an exhaustive set of facts and projections generated by his young staff. The weary Central Committee finally gave him the unanimous vote of confidence for which he had pressed them.

Next, Arnold held a series of meetings at the villages to present his plan to the whole population of the island. The members of the society were impressed by his programs to raise their standard of living and increase their leisure time. They were particularly enthusiastic about Arnold's goal, which was nothing less than a complete rejuvenation of their society. Arnold pointed out that the program would require a great deal of work and dedication. The more he asked of them, the more enthusiastic they became.

In addition to raising the standard of living, Arnold's goal featured a major buildup of the Ajax Island military capability. Arnold said that the island had fallen far behind in this respect. He contrasted their position with that of Comet Island, which had a standing army. Although the Comet Island army was small, Arnold pointed out that it could pose a considerable threat to Ajax Island, which had never had an army at all. Furthermore, he pointed out that the Comet Island industrial base was several times the size of the one on Ajax Island and capable of turning out armaments as much as ten times faster.

In his speeches, Arnold quoted from a book and several newspaper articles published on Comet Island, all of which argued that that society had a manifest destiny to expand its political system into other less well-favored places. He noted that people from Comet Island, under the guise of doing business, had been infiltrating Babo Island and had even made overtures to the management of the New Socratic Society. On Ajax Island, one of the parties had gone so far as to hint at something like a bribe. The ostensible purpose of these communications was strictly private and contemplated the building of factories on Ajax Island to be run by Comet Island managers to make products for export.

Arnold found it difficult to believe that the Comet Island government was not pulling the strings that operated these puppets. He pointed out that once such business people became established in an area, they would involve themselves in the local controversies that inevitably spring up, and their government—Comet Island, in this case, with its army—would then find some pretense to take over and annex the area. Arnold gave several examples where that had happened in other parts of the world. That train of events, he said, would lead to people from Comet Island imposing their system on Ajax Island and putting their own people in positions of authority.

With the backing of nearly everyone on the island, the new plan was put into effect and there was an immediate concentration on building up Ajax Island's industrial capacity. This included facilities for making all the basic armaments that Ajax Island needed. The armaments part of the program was given special priority and within a few years, enough had been produced to supply a sizable army.

While this was underway, Arnold instituted a broad program to train people in the various skills needed to defend their island. All of the men were made part of a militia, even the elderly and the infirm. The able-bodied drilled. Everyone in the militia studied tactics and the operation of various weapons. The women had classes also and practiced the various supporting roles. Even the children in the schools were trained to obey military orders immediately, to help in any way they might be asked, and to respect and honor the fighters. Tunnels were dug and hiding places constructed. As the military equipment was made available, the whole population went through defense drills in which a group portraying the invader landed on the beaches and moved inland.

Between the military and other aspects of the new program, the population was invigorated. Its efficiency even on mundane jobs improved substantially. Several years went by and Ajax Island remained in a state of readiness. Comet Island did nothing hostile, although several Comet Island businessmen came by and offered to act as agents to sell the output of the Ajax Island armament factories to other countries. Arnold had no trouble discerning the hand of the Comet Island government in their proposals. He was convinced that any such shipments of armaments would end up in stockpiles on Comet Island.

Two years later, Arnold and his staff noticed signs that the members were beginning to slip back into their old, somewhat indolent ways. They had begun to take the defense drills lightly and raise questions about converting the armament factories to making consumer goods.

After a considerable study of these new attitudes, the staff recommended that a smaller but especially well-equipped professional army be added to the militia. This could be promoted to the Ajax Islanders as a way of improving the defense system while relieving many of them of the need for such frequent military exercises. It would also impress upon the Comet Island government that the Ajax Island military force was now being equipped for offensive action. The staff argued that a good offense was known to be the best defense and Comet Island would see that even a hostile pass at Ajax Island might put the aggressor in serious danger. Furthermore, if Comet Island did invade, Ajax could mount its own counter-invasion.

Several more years were spent creating a well-trained professional army capable of effective military operations under any conditions. Arnold then began to make speeches on various occasions around Ajax Island in which he warned Comet Islanders that any aggressive action on their part would result in an immediate counterattack on Comet Island itself, one that could be devastating.

Nevertheless, life seemed to go on at Comet Island much as before, as though nothing of importance was happening on Ajax Island. From time to time, articles appeared in Comet Island newspapers reporting on the military preparedness of Ajax Island. In editorials the newspaper warned that Comet Island was falling behind and should devote more attention to modernizing its army. These sentiments were echoed in the legislature by two politicians. In one of the hearings, a witness brought up the benefits of a preemptive strike before the disparity in armed forces grew too great. This was widely quoted by Arnold in his speeches.

Two years later, a chieftain of one of the villages on Babo Island came to see Arnold with a long tale of problems and unfortunate events on his island. He claimed to be the legitimate heir to the position of high chief of the island by virtue of his pedigree. Unfortunately for him, politics had intervened and the council of chieftains had chosen another chieftain as high chief. The visiting chieftain spun a sordid tale of payoffs and promises. Men from Comet Island seeking trade concessions had made a deal with his rival and provided money to bribe the other chieftains.

He said that once elected, his rival had awarded the trading concessions as promised and the people from Comet Island built several trading posts on various parts of the island. They began to ply the Polynesians with liquor and run them into debt. Once having the upper hand, Comet Islanders began to buy up the land on Babo Island. Having legal title to much of the land, they began to overwork and mistreat the Polynesians and had been responsible for guards' beating several of the workers to death.

From the chieftain's point of view, the last straw came when the high chief signed over a sacred grove, a legacy in the chieftain's family, to a couple of Comet Islanders who planned to bring in a sawmill and cut down the trees for lumber. The chieftain had gone to Comet Island to appeal to the government there. The president, the leaders of the legislature, and the supreme court did not give him any satisfaction. They told him that they did not have the authority to deal with this since it was outside their territory; the government of Babo Island had jurisdiction. They emphasized that the Comet Island government had no control over the deals that Comet Island businessmen made when they were on Babo Island as long as they obeyed the Babo Island laws, which they appeared to be doing. A few of the Comet Island officials consoled the chieftain, and promised to talk to the businessmen, but could offer no assurance that anything would change.

Arnold was outraged. He sent two of his staff back to Babo Island with the chieftain to check on the matter. They returned with confirmation of the story. Arnold made a fiery speech on the subject, warning that the Polynesians on Babo Island had to be respected by Europeans and people living in European cultures. He pointed out that the Polynesians had settled on Babo Island long before the Europeans had reached either Comet or Ajax islands. Finally, he warned that interference with the way of life of the Polynesians on Babo Island, and certainly any destruction of the sacred grove, must not take place. If it did, the matter would be taken very seriously by the New Socratic Society. Arnold gave a copy of the speech to the Comet Island ambassador for transmittal to his president.

Two months later, the chieftain rushed back to Ajax Island and reported to Arnold that the sawmill had been completed and that the first sacred tree had been felled the day before and cut up into lumber. Arnold was livid. He sent for the Comet Island ambassador and told him to inform his government that Ajax Island would feel impelled to intervene unless Comet Island ceased interfering in the affairs of Babo Island.

Three days later, the ambassador informed Arnold that Comet Island was not involved in the matter and that Babo Island was the responsibility of its own sovereign government, which had a right to deal in any legitimate way it pleased with businessmen within its own territory. He further stated that Comet Island would do nothing to interfere with the operation of

Babo Island, and warned that his government would treat as very serious any interference by Ajax Island on Babo.

Two days later, the New Socratic Society marines and army landed on the west side of Babo Island with the assistance of the chieftain's village. The army fanned out quickly and gained control of the whole island. The high chief fled toward Comet Island and was not pursued. The army seized the Comet Island citizens who were on Babo Island and brought them together in a stockade, where they were confined under guard, but were otherwise well treated. The army quickly fortified the harbors on Babo Island and settled down to await any action that Comet Island might chose to take. Thus far there had been no bloodshed.

The Comet Island ambassador presented a strongly worded protest to Arnold. There were protest meetings held in the Comet Island city and each of the villages. A special session of the Comet Island legislature was held, at which most of the discussion centered on how to win release of the Comet Island citizens. The president's office on Comet Island held round-the-clock strategy sessions. Newspapers called for an immediate counterstrike against Ajax Island. The Comet Island army was beseiged by volunteers. The legislature appropriated money to modernize the army's equipment and to build up the stockpiles of ammunition.

Despite all indications that public opinion was solidly behind an aggressive response to the Ajax Island action, it was evident to everyone in the Comet Island government that the Ajax army and navy were much better equipped and trained than any force Comet Island could send against them. Further, it did not seem possible to make Comet Island militarily competitive in less than two years.

The president of Comet Island made a formal offer to withhold any armed retaliation, provided Comet Island and Ajax Island sat down and negotiated all the questions concerning Babo Island to settle their respective relationships with that island in a way that would be fair to everyone, particularly the inhabitants of Babo Island. After several discussions and diplomatic letters back and forth, Arnold accepted the proposal when Comet Island agreed to his demand that the meetings be held in the sacred grove on Babo Island.

The negotiations dragged on for six months. As agreed, most of the time there were no official reports on where the negotiations stood and what points were still in disagreement. The people on Comet Island got more and more upset about the continued holding of their citizens on Babo Island, even though the detention of their compatriots had been one of the Ajax Island conditions to which Comet Island had agreed.

The Comet Islanders were annoyed with their government and pressed it to bring the negotiations to a speedy conclusion and obtain the release of people they regarded as hostages.

Finally, the representatives of Ajax Island and Comet Island reached an agreement that included the prompt return of all Comet Island citizens seized on Babo Island. It was agreed that there should be a conference among the chieftains on Babo Island, with observers from both Ajax Island and Comet Island. The chieftains would again elect a high chief and decide the conditions under which the inhabitants of Babo Island wished to live. The governments of both Ajax Island and Comet Island agreed to respect the wishes of the Babo Island inhabitants.

The original high chief objected strongly to these arrangements. However, he had been protesting loudly at every opportunity since he fled the island. The people on Comet Island told him to go back to Babo Island and rally his supporters. He refused, saying that as long as the Ajax Island military remained in control of the island, he would fear for his life if he were to return. It was true that the Ajax Island military personnel put pressure on the chieftains to vote the way Ajax Island thought best and there were a few isolated instances of such pressure reported in the Comet Island newspapers. However, the newspapers could only conjecture as to the extent of this activity, and the Comet Islanders were not interested in hearing about it.

After several sessions that were mostly ceremonial in nature, the chieftains reelected their current high chief and agreed unanimously that they wished to continue running the island as a protectorate of the New Socratic Society. A year later, after further hostile articles in the Comet Island newspapers and some critical speeches in the legislature, Arnold, with the high chief at his side, announced that in order to forestall action threatened by Comet Island, the chieftains had asked that Babo Island be integrated completely into the New Socratic Society. Arnold proudly announced that the society governing both Ajax and Babo islands would henceforth be known as the NSS Republic.

In the next several years there was a substantial reorganization of the NSS Republic. Half the members of the society on Ajax Island were moved into new villages built for them on Babo Island. The announced intention was to move half the Polynesians to Ajax Island, but they objected strongly, and only about ten percent were induced to go. Initially they were moved into the apartments vacated by the members who moved to Babo Island. However, the Polynesians did not like apartment living and were granted the right to build their own villages, which included living quarters similar to those on Babo Island.

Arnold's intention was to integrate the two populations. A number of practical problems prevented this. The program was based on the assumption that the Polynesians would fit into a European management structure, but they were unwilling to do so. Consequently the Polynesians wound up working in groups largely composed of their own people and generally these groups did unskilled work. This resulted in the Polynesians being paid less than the Europeans. This was not a problem to them since necessities were still low-priced and the Polynesians were not interested in buying most of the other goods that the managers chose to have the stores carry.

Arnold was disappointed that the society did not homogenize more rapidly; he reluctantly concluded that Polynesians were not going to assimilate until they had mastered the NSS culture as children by progressing through the school system. After a few years, it became obvious that this would take a while, since most of the Polynesian children did not do well in the NSS schools. On top of this, there seemed to be *sub rosa* resistance from his own managers to his directions that they give the Polynesians special attention in order to speed up their acculturation.

Not all the Polynesians were satisfied with their treatment in the NSS Republic. A steady trickle found their way over to Comet Island where they settled on the north shore in a Polynesian enclave headed by the former high chief, who continued his agitation to be reinstated on Babo Island and to have it restored to an independent island run by Polynesians. His supporters collected money from sympathetic Comet Islanders and accumulated a substantial arsenal of weapons. They organized a private militia and conducted amphibious landing exercises.

A new president took office on Comet Island and included in his state-of-the-island speech a pledge to work for the liberation of Babo Island. Ajax Islanders who visited Comet Island kept an eye on the Polynesian enclave and noted a substantial buildup of activity. The Comet Island army was sending in units to train the Polynesians and was supplying them with modern weapons.

Some months later, there was an invasion of Babo Island by the Polynesian supporters of the former high chief. The landings were made in an area guarded by men of the former high chief's village who were later executed as traitors. It was a cloudy night with no moonlight when the armada of small boats from Comet Island landed. The Ajax Island navy had long been expecting such an adventure and observed the force moving along. They passed the word on to their land forces, who permitted the invaders to penetrate a mile into Babo Island before ambushing them. About half the invaders were killed or captured, but the rest managed to get back to their boats.

Each boat for itself, they fled back to their base on Comet Island. The NSS navy attempted to sink the boats as they fled. Most of them got through until they neared Comet Island. Suddenly the cloud cover broke and the moon lit up the area, showing everyone the location of the other vessels. The NSS ships began firing rapidly, sinking one boat after another. At that point, the fight was close to shore and within the Comet Island territorial waters. Suddenly the shore batteries on a headland opened fire on the NSS warships.

The NSS ships suffered substantial casualties. They turned their attention to the shore batteries and fired at them. Then they landed marines who assaulted the batteries and put them out of action. When the sun came up, the NSS marines were holding a two-mile beachhead including the headland on the north shore of Comet Island. The NSS navy brought more ships to the scene and landed a regiment of their army. For several days, there was almost no organized resistance from the Comet Island army and no serious attempt to dislodge the NSS troops.

Arnold and members of his staff steamed to the scene and then reported back to the Central Committee that Comet Island appeared to be much weaker that they had suspected. He attributed this to their decadent society. He told the Central Committee that, after much soul searching, he had decided to ask their support for a plan to send in most of the army. The Ajax Island military had developed plans for invading Comet Island several years before and had pulled out recently revised versions from their files. Arnold pointed out that there were many reasons for the Tidy Isles to be united under one government and that this was an opportunity to settle the matter with minimum loss of life. The Central Committee voted unanimously to support him.

By the time the NSS army had established itself on Comet Island, it was opposed by the full Comet Island army. Nevertheless, the NSS army was larger, better equipped, better trained, and had the benefit of a well-thought-out battle plan. After a short battle, the NSS army broke through the Comet Island lines on both the east and west sides and moved south down the island.

While the NSS army was still strung out across the northern third of Comet Island, its leading units suddenly ran into a zone of bitter resistance. Remnants of the Comet Island army, armed civilians, and, most of all, the terrain combined to bring the NSS army to a halt. On both the east and west sides at this part of the island, there were marshes at the shore and large gorges running down to the coast; a precipitous part of the mountain blocked the area in between.

The NSS forces tried going around by water, but were repelled. They tried direct frontal assaults on various parts of the line, but were thrown back each time. The casualties were mounting. Finally, Arnold ordered a respite and proposed a diplomatic settlement to the Comet Island president. He pointed out the perilous position of the Comet Island forces, and explained that for many obvious reasons it would be desirable for the Tidy Isles to act as one united body. Arnold disclaimed any intention of depriving the Comet Islanders of their standard of living or their culture, and he promised them autonomy within the overall structure of the NSS Republic.

Discussions were initiated between representatives of the NSS and the Comet Island governments. These went on for several months with neither side willing to make substantial concessions. Arnold ordered a resumption of the offensive. The NSS army brought in more troops and supplies and prepared to move out against the Comet Island positions. The night before this was to have happened, a regiment of the Comet Island army burst out from the precipitous walls of the mountain, having lowered themselves from the top, and overran the NSS positions in the east. The next morning, the main force of the Comet Island army moved across the NSS trenches on the east side and struck quickly to the north.

The NSS army retired to the north to keep their troops from being outflanked and took up positions on a defense line which left it occupying the northern fifth of Comet Island. The Comet Island army moved up opposite the NSS positions and both sides dug in. Neither was able to make a meaningful breach in the line of the other and the two armies were left facing each other along increasingly fortified positions.

At the time of the original landing, the NSS navy had instituted a blockade of Comet Island. The blockade no doubt reduced Comet Island's ability to trade, but ways were found to get shipments in and out of the island as necessary. Some of the Comet Island commercial ships were faster than anything in the NSS navy. As a result, the government of Comet Island was able to maintain a substantial level of exports and accumulate monetary credits on the mainland.

After the stalemate between the armies had gone on for over a year, a new Comet Island navy suddenly appeared, manned and commanded mainly by mercenaries. The ships had been built for Comet Island on the mainland and were accompanied by warships from a mainland country allied with Comet Island. Together, these constituted a force greater than the NSS navy. In the ensuing battle, more than half the NSS ships were sunk or captured and the remainder wound up anchored in the only fortified harbor on Ajax Island.

The tables had been turned. The Comet Island navy blockaded both Babo and Ajax islands and was able to cut off most shipments of supplies to the NSS troops on Comet Island. After six months, the NSS army had been reduced to short rations of food, ammunition, medical supplies, fuel, etc. Then, on a stormy night, the Comet Island navy conducted a raid on the harbor in Ajax Island and destroyed most of the remaining NSS ships. Comet Island amphibious forces began to conduct raids on both Ajax and Babo Islands. The NSS troops started to desert and go over to the Comet Island side.

The top management of the NSS had gradually become quite rigid, with all the power concentrated in Arnold's hands. Nothing could be initiated without his personal permission. Several members of the Central Committee who opposed him on specific issues were tried, convicted, and executed as traitors. After that, there were no dissenting voices on the committee.

Nevertheless, in light of developments taking place in the war, some of the younger members of the Central Committee, members who had been newly appointed by Arnold himself, began to talk secretly among themselves about withdrawing from Comet Island. It appeared to them that they were about to lose the war, with consequences that might be disastrous. It also appeared to them that merely being involved in the war had wrecked their whole pattern of living. They felt that any gains from winning the war, even if this were possible, could not offset the damage being done.

They carefully tested the attitudes of each of the older members of the committee and concluded that none of them wanted to continue the war. Finally, they brought the subject up to Arnold in a very deferential way. Arnold stormed off and the committee members feared the worst. However, a week later he brought the matter up in the Central Committee meeting and asked for a secret ballot. Arnold said he was neutral and would refrain from voting. The result was a unanimous vote for withdrawal.

Arnold reluctantly accepted the committee's wishes and directed that they be put into effect. An emissary was sent to the president of Comet Island to convey an offer to withdraw all the NSS troops. The NSS Republic agreed not to threaten the sovereignty of Comet Island and not to permit itself to be used as a base for any future attack on Comet Island, provided Comet Island would agree to do the same. The NSS also proposed that the two nations sign a mutual defense treaty guaranteeing assistance if either nation were attacked from any other quarter.

The legislature on Comet Island debated this offer at great length, in the end advising the president to accept it. The president had reached the same conclusion, and not long thereafter the Tidy Isles war was over.

Arnold continued as leader while the NSS rebuilt its economy and worked to restore as much of the previous culture as it could. He died in office five years later, reportedly of natural causes.

The NSS Republic has evolved in the decades since then; there have been no further wars and no changes in the state's boundaries. The management, since Arnold's death, has been firmly in the hands of the Central Committee, whose members have continued to elect the leader. They have permitted none of these to have the kind of dictatorial power that Arnold enjoyed. Most of the leaders have been past middle age and some have even been elderly. The primary interest they and the members of the Central Committee have displayed has been a desire to preserve the status quo.

Nevertheless, the NSS Republic has changed, along with the rest of the world. It has maintained a small but well-trained military force at all times, and has continued the program of training all citizens in military skills, particularly in the schools. The children have also been indoctrinated by learning a nationalistic and heroic version of NSS history.

The NSS Republic has been somewhat slow to introduce new technology. However, when management felt sure that a new technology was sufficiently mature and was confident that its experts could select the right equipment, then management has purchased, installed, and used the technology. The members of NSS management have been well aware that they often lagged behind other countries in the adoption of new technology, but they note instances around the world where other countries have committed themselves too soon only to find that they had to abandon the technology or purchase substitute equipment.

At the time the NSS Republic was formed, the Polynesian and European populations were approximately the same size. The total population has grown considerably since then, but the Polynesians have had bigger families and their numbers have come to predominate. About eighty percent of the population is Polynesian, ten percent mixed, and ten percent European. The Polynesians have stubbornly continued to live largely in their old culture, although they gradually made the transition from their huts to some rather temporary-looking one-story housing. Those of mixed blood live with the Europeans in the regular apartments, although as a group they have never been accepted as full equals.

A visitor today might well view the NSS as a bit grim. Perhaps this reflects the management prejudice against bright colors, signs and advertising, showy flowering trees, and any sort of individual display that invites attention. The facial expressions of the European NSS citizens one sees on the street are not open, never suggest they are having fun, and generally show the opposite of ebullience. Rather, they appear as a serious people, possibly a bit dull, who are going about the business of doing what they have a duty to do. The Polynesians may be another matter, but it is difficult to tell because they are always reserved in the presence of a visitor. In addition, NSS rules prohibit visitors to the islands from entering the Polynesian villages.

The descendants of the Europeans, even those of low rank, live in comfortable apartments, eat healthful foods selected by the managers for the farmers to grow and the stores to carry, and send their children to schools with impressive curricula. The people are not encouraged to be creative, and the schooling relies heavily on memorizing approved materials. These NSS members read about twice as many books per year as do inhabitants on Comet Island and they still engage in philosophical discussions during a month-long annual celebration of the original landing.

The Polynesian dwellings are packed together in dense clusters. The walls are thin and the odors from each house are blown out into the walkways. All the building entrances are visible from several other buildings. Unlike the regular NSS apartments, the living units are smaller and there is less furniture. Everything about these villages bespeaks lower cost.

A closer look also shows that everything has been constructed so that there is practically no privacy. This is not inconsistent with Polynesian culture, and it happens to fit the interests of the Central Committee, too. There are numerous informers among the Polynesians, and this, together with the lack of privacy, makes it very difficult to organize any subversive activities. In fact, there never has been a successful attempt to develop a group of Polynesian dissidents of any significant size.

Living accommodations are better for those with higher status in the society. At the top, the members of the Central Committee have large houses with servants. They enjoy trips abroad at regular intervals and their children are taught in special schools equipped with more and better teachers and books. The Central Committee members also get paid considerably more than anyone else in the society and have access to a private stock of imported goods.

The members of the Central Committee feel no need to apologize for the things they enjoy. They have worked hard, disciplined themselves, and have been lucky; they deserve what they have been awarded. Central Committee members happen also to have the authority to make these awards to each other. They understand how important it is to the society that Central Committee members, who make the most crucial decisions, be firmly wedded to the system. If any members of the Central Committee were to try to desert and live in a free society somewhere, they and their families would be tracked down and killed wherever they might hide. No such action has ever been necessary.

By law, the job assignments are distributed strictly on the basis of merit, and these largely determine a member's status in the society for other purposes. All Polynesians essentially work at menial jobs. They do not profit much from school and do not seem able to learn the NSS system of doing things. They grumble that their schools have fewer and poorer teachers, which is true. However, the society has been integrated for over a hundred years and generation after generation of the Polynesians have had the opportunity to rise up through the system if they so desired. The managers can only conclude that most of them are satisfied with their way of life and unwilling to make the extra effort. No Polynesian has ever been a member of the Central Committee, although there has been one member of mixed blood.

Actually, the managers think Polynesians make out very well, considering their minimal contributions. They are adequately fed, housed, and clothed and receive standard medical service. They are encouraged to go on with many aspects of their Polynesian culture. Most of the things they do not participate in, such as travel or intellectual stimulation, are things they would not want anyway.

There are, of course, occasional Europeans who are not up to the technical demands of managerial jobs. Because they come from families who are used to having their children do well, the family pushes them to the full extent of their capabilities. Fundamentally, however, the family handles these cases by using favors. All the managers ask for favors from one another and repay in kind. They function in an unofficial network to solve a variety of problems by such a mechanism. Typically, through this mechanism a dull young man or woman of the managerial class is placed in a respectable, but undemanding white-collar job which ranks as having managerial status.

The members of the NSS Republic live in a very stable nation in which everyone is cared for, has the opportunity to live a life of dignity and comfort and to be a benefit to humanity. In the beginning, there were people leaving the society for the mainland and even for Comet Island. This no longer happens. The dissatisfied are encouraged to bring their complaints to the managers, who will handle them carefully. There is very little crime and the NSS corrective institutions are mainly occupied with people who need help in achieving a change of attitude. It is not always easy to predict how long it will take for people to change their attitudes; in some cases, it is not completed in a lifetime.

14

The Heavily Modified Status Society

CHARACTERISTICS OF OLIGARCHIES

The society had existed for a hundred and fifty years on Ajax Island with one continuous line of governance. All this time, its foundation was a network of status-society rules. During this long period, however, there occurred significant changes in the rules and the way the society functioned. Beginning in Albert's time, the rules incorporated many free-society features. In later times, the rules evolved further until Andrew's principles, such as strict avoidance of personal motivation in making societal decisions, while still held up as ideals, were no longer inviolate in everyday practice.

For most of this hundred-and-fifty-year period, the island was run by an oligarchy, comprising essentially the members of the Central Committee. Most status societies, primary or secondary, that have a multigenerational line of governance passing smoothly from one leader to another over a long period, seem to utilize the oligarchic form of leadership, whether they are sovereign states, churches, businesses, or whatever.

Oligarchies are notoriously conservative. The members of the governing body have the best, most comfortable, most powerful positions in their society and therefore much to defend. The members of the Central Committee were heads of the departments of the government and had a reasonably free hand in running their baronies. These positions provided them with the necessary power base to function as members of the oligarchy. They would go to extreme lengths to protect these positions. This, too, is characteristic of oligarchies. The members of the ruling group are roughly

135

equivalent, by virtue of their being members and department heads, and are in similar positions in that they are subject to many of the same pressures. Consequently, each member of the oligarchy shares many common values with the others. Indeed, the group resists the addition of a new member unless it is comfortable with the person, knows he or she identifies with the group's values and is confident that it can predict the person's behavior. The group members must all be ready to stand united when they are under pressure and need to protect their positions. Thus the group is naturally of one mind on most subjects.

In normal circumstances one of the members of the oligarchy is designated by the group as its leader and is given control over the actions of the other members and through them the society. However, there are tacitly understood limits to how much the leader may interfere with any particular member's barony; the members get very touchy when the leader threatens to go beyond these boundaries. Part of the oligarchy game is for the group to hold back enough authority so that it can overturn any leader who goes too far. Leaders, for their part, try to get enough power to restructure the group if it balks at carrying out their program.

The other members of the society have much less power, and in various ways enjoy a lower standard of living than members of the oligarchy. This discrepancy is maintained, in part, as a mechanism to emphasize the difference in status. It helps to keep the society under control. The oligarchy recognizes that increases in the standard of living for ordinary members of society often stimulate the demand for more increases. Worse yet, an increase in the standard of living that has to be withdrawn later is dangerous and can trigger violence. In like manner, concessions in the form of freedoms for ordinary members of society clearly tend to increase levels of dissatisfaction thereby increasing the risk that the members will demand the freedoms people have in some neighboring free society.

The oligarchy depends on the loyal support of those in the next lower rungs of management, i.e., the middle managers. It is normal to give these managers substantially more benefits than ordinary members so that they will have a stronger personal stake in preserving the system. One of the mechanisms often used for this is to permit the middle managers to do favors for themselves and their colleagues.

The middle managers are the main group of society members who are in positions to do favors. Most of the decisions a manager makes in such societies should be unbiased and in accordance with the requirements of the rules. The decisions that are influenced by the desire to do a favor should be exceptions. However, if there are enough decision-requiring steps in each problem, there will be room for an exception somewhere along the line in most cases.

The members of the oligarchy, knowing that favors are being given, insist that the middle managers maintain the appearance of making unbiased decisions. The oligarchy and the middle managers have a tacit understanding of which circumstances permit the granting of a favor and which do not. One advantage of this system for the oligarchy is that ordinary members of the society will blame the managers rather than the oligarchy for the corruption under these circumstances.

The ordinary members get fewer benefits, but even here, some inherent status differences are commonly embedded in the system. In the NSS Republic, the Europeans were given the white-collar or specialist jobs; those of mixed race were typically foremen. The Polynesians were relegated to the blue-collar jobs. Of course, there were individual differences based on merit, but, on average, such merit distinctions were small relative to the distinctions between ethnic groups.

The upshot is that there are usually few public expressions of dissatisfaction in a reasonably well-run oligarchy. The system has gone on for many years; people know where they stand, and they feel that struggling against the system is futile. In the NSS it was possible for a member to advance, but rarely more than one rung up the ladder in a lifetime. Fundamentally, the oligarchy tries to provide whatever benefits are needed, neither more nor less, to keep each group pacified.

The oligarchic form of government can be very stable and effective in controlling a society. The operation of an oligarchy involves giving the leaders special privileges that are not available to the average member. How the oligarchy chooses to run other aspects of the society can vary. There are modes that range from having the government decide what is good for members, to letting the members buy what they want, to permitting the whole area of economic activity to be run under free-society rules, with or without government intervention to promote growth in particular directions.

The requirement of the status-society ethical principle that government judge every action by what produces the most overall good is typically drowned out in the oligarchic societies by the lines of power distribution required in this type of government. Since the government can be very powerful, the virtue of the society depends on the character and ambition of its leaders.

HEAVILY MODIFIED STATUS SOCIETIES

In addition to oligarchies, such as the one on Ajax Island, there are many other types of heavily modified status societies. Many of them are not oligarchies, and some may even be democracies. Commonly, however, these societies are governed by some form of dictatorship. Such governments do not usually have the longevity of the oligarchies, but their basic nature may change little from one dictator to the next.

Another form of status society is based on a religion. Religions may vary considerably but they share the goal of creating a society that objectifies the religion. There seem also to have been heavily modified status societies that were held together by bonds of custom, perhaps supported by a shared religion.

Few modern societies would seem to have any close resemblance to either the pure status society or pure free society. In the heavily modified forms it is sometimes difficult to characterize the foundation network of rules since, in terms of their effect on people's actions, there are so many of both kinds of rules. However, one can often perceive a group of underlying network rules that set the fundamental overriding way in which the society operates.

One indication that a state is a modified status society is that to the extent citizens have rights against the government they are rights to have the government give them benefits. In the corresponding heavily modified free society they are fundamentally rights to exclude the government from the citizens' individual spheres of choice.

Another indication is whether the government gives priority to an overall societal goal other than the welfare of its citizens. Examples are expanding the territory of the state or building a dutiful religious society. Overall positive objectives of this sort would indicate some form of status society. A government that is carried along on the tide of individual private actions and ambitions indicates some variety of free society.

This is not to argue that every state must necessarily be classified as some form of either status society or free society. The two types of rules may be so admixed and entwined that the naming of the society as one or the other becomes a meaningless formality. This does not mean, however, that the ways in which the rules work and the ethical principles involved are any less pertinent than in any other society.

The government of a status society has much more power than the government of a free society. Thus, in cases where a dictator is able to seize control of a state, he or she will nearly always set up a form of modified status society. Typically such a government is not broadly concerned with the welfare of its citizens, except as needed to stay in power. Ethical principles often do not play much of a role in drafting the rules.

It is important to notice the similarity and difference between the rationale for the dictatorial state and a dictatorial business. Both organizations are fundamentally status societies. The benefits offered to the citizens of the state and to the employees of the business are often the minimum that the respective leaders feel they can provide without disrupting the organization. The standard by which the leaders judge the rules in both cases is benefit to the leaders.

The essential difference is that the state is a primary society and the business is a secondary society. The former compels its members to do things by threat of force, while the latter does not have that power. For the citizens there is little alternative to following the orders of the state. For the employees, there is the alternative of finding another job in a competitive marketplace or starting their own businesses. These alternatives may not be attractive, but that is a matter of capabilities, not of rights. The key difference is that employees are in their positions after the opportunity to bargain to an agreement, the citizen is not. It is this that makes such a dictator's goals contrary to societal-ethics principles while the business leader's goals will typically be in accordance with personal-ethics principles. Although the approaches are the same, one is a primary society and calls for societal ethics; the other is a secondary society for which personal ethics are appropriate.

15

A Welfare State

With the adoption of its constitution a hundred and forty years ago, Comet Island became a democratic sovereign state. Since then, the world and Comet Island have gone through many changes. Economically the island has flourished. Starting as an agricultural state, it followed the lead of the United States, Europe, and Japan and evolved into a predominantly industrial society.

The village at the south end of the island, which early on became the largest population center, grew into a city. It has continued to grow, becoming surrounded by suburbs. Today its metropolitan area contains about half the Comet Island population.

In contrast, the area devoted to agriculture initially grew with the population, but peaked around the year 1900 and has declined ever since. With its large urban population, the island has not, for many years, produced enough food to sustain itself. Government planners have calculated that with a proper choice of crops and the cultivation of every nook and cranny, Comet Island could produce enough food to scrape by in an emergency.

Nevertheless, emotional ties to an agricultural past and the old fear of a blockade of its ports influence the psychology of the inhabitants of Comet Island. The government subsidizes farming and restricts farm owners from going out of business. In a curious, but logical development, recently passed laws require that a farm have an attractive appearance in order to receive its subsidy. Picturesque farm country, it seems, attracts tourists with cameras.

Metropolitan growth has come in spurts. In the beginning, growth in the city was unregulated, streets were narrow, and the sanitation system primitive (not unusual for the time). After a number of decades, the old part of town, down by the harbor, became undesirable as a neighborhood for those who could afford better. As the city expanded, affluent city dwellers moved into new houses in the outlying areas, while arriving immigrants moved into the older, poorer housing. After a few more decades, industries moved into the harbor area and tore down the houses, replacing them with factories and warehouses.

For many years after, the harbor area was a bustling manufacturing location. But then the industries around the harbor fell on hard times and the buildings deteriorated. The subsequent generations of new factories have been located mainly in the suburbs. The harbor area was rescued two decades ago by a wave of renewal in which the old industrial buildings were torn down and modified or replaced to produce an area of office-apartment complexes interspersed with hotels, boutiques, and fashionable restaurants.

The city government required the builders of these new complexes to restore various remnants of earlier structures, running all the way back to the original village by the shore. There is even a park that claims to preserve the spot where the first president, Henry, originally landed on the island and dragged his boat up on the sand. The harbor area appears to be settling into another pleasant middle age. Unfortunately, to some it looks a bit sterile. Nothing is being built. In fact, current land-use regulations make new commercial construction economically unfeasible.

From the first, a substantial portion of the new Comet Island population had been fairly recent immigrants. The earliest ones came from western Europe. Many of them married Polynesians, and the oldest families on the island are proud of their Polynesian heritage. The particular Polynesians they are descended from are claimed to be a different, more heroic tribe than the Polynesians who remained on Babo Island and those who immigrated later from other parts of the Pacific. Other waves of immigrants came from eastern and southern Europe, China, and at various times groups from South America. Quite recently, there have been immigrants from Southeast Asia.

The long period of commercial and industrial development was interrupted by the most traumatic episode in Comet Island history. The NSS Republic had chosen the notorious dictator Arnold as its leader. The Comet Island army warned that he had embarked on a course of militarization. The army had demanded a very large increase in funding to rebuild itself after the government's inattention to it during the preceding decades of peace. People were skeptical. The Liberals were in power at the time and they increased army appropriations by twenty percent instead of the two thousand percent requested. Liberal party leaders visited Ajax Island and talked with Arnold. They reported back that he was a very capable executive with a wide range of progressive ideas and programs; if Comet Island left him alone, he would leave them alone.

Then the NSS seized Babo Island, shocking the Comet Island population, which now viewed Ajax Island as an immediate threat. Many Comet Islanders wanted to declare war and settle the matter. They pointed out that Comet Island had a substantially larger population, a well-established standing army, and, most important, a much greater industrial capacity. Cooler heads prevailed. The matter was left to diplomatic negotiation, which dragged on for a number of months. Gradually the Comet Island population lost interest in most aspects of the episode, although they became more and more insistent on the retrieval of their own citizens who had been caught on the island by the invasion and were being interned.

Finally, some of the radical members of the Liberal party took matters into their own hands and visited Ajax Island to hear Arnold's side of the story. He pointed out that Babo Island was a totally undeveloped society in need of help; that the high chief had appealed to Comet Island but had been ignored. His appeal to Ajax Island was not something Arnold could, in good conscience, deny. All the NSS had done was to send in emergency assistance on a temporary basis.

The radicals came back to Comet Island well satisfied with these explanations and forced the government's hand. As a result, the Comet Island government agreed to a settlement with Arnold, which rescued the Comet Island citizens but gave in on nearly all other points of contention.

A year later, the NSS formally annexed Babo Island and began inducting the Polynesians into its army. The Conservatives on Comet Island made dire predictions. They were returned to power in the next election, with a mandate to strengthen the island's defenses. The Conservatives proposed and passed an ambitious program to do this, raising money through tax increases and cuts in government services.

Long before the next election, the population became bored with the military program, grew weary of the new taxes, and complained insistently about the diminished services. Things were quiet on Ajax and Babo islands. The Comet Island voters elected a Liberal president who claimed that he would be tough on the NSS, but would, at the same time, drastically reduce the military program expenditures, cut taxes, and increase services.

Some months later, the NSS, on the thinnest of excuses, invaded

Comet Island itself. With overwhelming support, the Liberals set aside the constitution, assumed extraordinary powers, and during the rest of their term of office did what they felt was necessary to win the war.

At first the war did not go well. The NSS army conquered the northern third of the island, pushing back the smaller, less well-equipped Comet Island standing army. It was evident that the money spent by the Conservatives on the military had been used largely to build an industrial base and infrastructure. The benefits of that program had not yet flowed through to the combat troops. Even rifles and ammunition were in short supply.

The army was bolstered by a rush of volunteers from all over the island. Unfortunately, these were predominantly factory workers, not the hunters, farmers, and sailors of earlier years. Their lack of training and experience was costly.

Stopping the NSS advance was accomplished by extraordinary heroism and skillful use of the terrain. While the invaders were held up at the battle line for several months, the Comet Island government bought, borrowed, and manufactured arms and ammunition. The turning point came when Horace, the war's best-known hero, led a hand-picked group of volunteers on a nighttime climb around the mountain, rappelling down a cliff behind the enemy positions. The group attacked the NSS lines from behind, breaching them in the east. The next morning, Comet Island troops poured through the open salient and the NSS army had to retreat quickly to avoid being surrounded. The NSS Republic was able to stabilize its line at a point that left it in control of the northern fifth of Comet Island. Both sides dug in, laid mines, and settled down to a seige.

The war dragged on in a stalemate. Conservatives won the next election by promising to run the war effectively. Once in power they recognized that a frontal assault on the NSS lines would cost an excessive number of lives and was out of the question. They also recognized that the Comet Island superiority lay in its industrial and financial power. In the Conservatives' view, this could be most advantageously used to fight the war at sea. Over the next few months, Comet Island had a fleet of warships built for them by allies on the mainland. The new fleet steamed out to lift the blockade, and in the ensuing battle destroyed most of the NSS navy. Comet Island then set up a blockade of the NSS, trying particularly to interrupt supply shipments to the NSS troops on Comet Island.

The Conservatives finally reached a peace settlement with the NSS Republic, perhaps partly because of a little-known arrangement Arnold talked them into, under which Comet Island provided a subsidy to the

NSS to help rebuild its economy. The relationship with the NSS has continued with civility since then. In fact, several decades later, the Liberals were saying that Comet Island could learn quite a bit from the way in which the NSS got things done. They pointed out that there was never any unemployment, and no one was homeless or went hungry. They pressed to have some of the NSS features built into the system on Comet Island.

In the years since, the voters have swung back and forth between the Liberals and Conservatives, electing them to power more or less alternately. The Liberals have initiated regulatory and public service programs, including laws establishing minimum wages and restricting terms of employment. The Conservatives have responded with tax-reduction programs, real-estate zoning, and land-planning measures.

One of the Conservative reforms improved the legal status of women. On Comet Island, women had always provided leadership in the arts, charities, medical care, and so forth. They had also played an important role running commercial enterprises. In fact, on average, women had more important roles on Comet Island than on Ajax Island. Nevertheless, the NSS women had the same legal status as men, whereas the Comet Island women, to their annoyance, were second-class citizens; they weren't even allowed to vote. The new laws gave them the same rights as men. This conflicted with some of the earlier Liberal legislation that, to protect women's health, restricted the jobs in which women could be employed. Both sets of laws are still on the books and nobody has been able to force the courts or the legislature to settle the apparent conflict.

Generally, when the Conservatives were in power, economic growth surged. On at least one occasion, it may have surged too much. A couple of decades after the war, the Conservatives got the economy going very strongly. The prices of real estate and shares of stock both rose much higher than cautious investors could justify. Those who owned the right properties became wealthy. There were stories of unsophisticated workers buying stocks or playing the commodity market and making fortunes overnight.

Shortly thereafter, the economy suffered a severe crash, followed by a depression. During the worst part of those troubled times a third of the wage earners were jobless. The Conservatives seemed paralyzed. They provided food and shelter and waited for the situation to turn around. The economy did improve, but it was still very weak when the next election brought the Liberals back to power.

Taxes were raised again and made very progressive. Taxes on tobacco, liquor, and automobiles were instituted not only to raise more money but to further the government's goal of reducing the use of these items for the good of the users. Welfare grants were established to provide a living for various categories of people who were not sustaining themselves economically.

In the early days on Comet Island, each family had been responsible for its own welfare. Where help was given, it came from neighbors or personal friends who were involved with the recipient. As the society became bigger and more affluent, people began to feel that the needy should be helped in a more organized way, so they developed charities. During the depression, the charities were overwhelmed. The government stepped in to take on the job, setting up an attendant bureacracy to do it.

At first, the assistance was limited to necessities. But, as with many temporary emergency measures, the bureacracy continued to expand its work in good times and bad. The definition of what constituted need was gradually extended to cover everyone living below an income level viewed as the tolerable minimum.

With the Liberals running the country, the economy remained in convalescence for a number of years. The Conservatives said the continued economic weakness was because the government was spending too much money and the very high progressive tax rates were leaving people little incentive to work, to take risks, or to produce incremental income. The Liberals attributed the weak economy to the government's unwillingness to spend enough and to the private sector's failure to get its job done. Finally, the voters decided to try the Conservatives again.

In recent years, the Liberals have gradually lost the support of the average voter, but they have learned to be sensitive to special-interest groups. These groups want something specific and show the ability to deliver votes to the party that gets it for them.

An early special-interest group consisted of the Polynesians who had escaped in later years from the NSS and settled in an enclave on the north coast of Comet Island. Even after many decades there, they had not assimilated into the Comet Island culture and they averaged much lower incomes than the rest of the population. The Liberals espoused the theory that these people were entitled to special help as full-blooded descendants of the first settlers on the Tidy Isles. They passed laws requiring that all employers hire a certain percentage of full-blooded Polynesians.

Some employers did find assimilated Polynesians to hire. Others had various problems. In many cases jobs were located too far from the enclave for the Polynesians to commute, and inhabitants of the enclave would not move out into the rest of the island. The law was not enforced in such cases, but it was not modified either. The government built low-rent housing near the enclave and gave preference to the full-blooded Polynesians in renting the units.

When the Conservatives regained power, they spent less money on the Liberal programs, but they did not dare eliminate them. They did reduce taxes, however. When the Liberals got back in, they concentrated on putting into place new programs that would appeal to new special-interest groups and would bring in new voters. Then, as their programs caused inflation, the Liberals created protective restrictions, including rent control and temporary full-blown price-control programs.

Price controls thoroughly disrupted the island's economy; they were ended when the Conservatives were voted back into office. The Conservatives were not so bold as to eliminate rent control, however. Instead, they cut taxes and the economy improved. Nevertheless, the overall economy on Comet Island has been losing vigor in the last several decades. On the average, about ten percent of the work force is unemployed and living on job insurance; another ten percent of the population lives on welfare.

By law, jobs on Comet Island are regulated so as to pay high wages and include attractive fringe benefits. Unfortunately it is not easy to get a regulated job. Most young workers can find only temporary, unregulated jobs working for small employers. The terms of such employment are not in writing and invariably include provisions that are illegal. If reported to the authorities, the job merely disappears within the next two weeks. (The government has to give two weeks' notice before it is permitted to investigate, and if the job is no longer in existence, the investigation is canceled.) Small employers are not punished for past transgressions, because they, too, are a well-organized political force with representation in both Conservative and Liberal parties.

It has become almost impossible to find rental housing. None has been built for several decades, with the exception of the government-built, low-rent housing. These low-rent apartment buildings are dominated by gangs; only those who cannot avoid it live in them.

Very little land changes hands. Taxes on real estate are low, courtesy of the real-estate owners' special-interest group, so people are not under pressure to sell. At the same time, it takes so many layers of government approval to change the authorized use of a piece of land that buyers cannot afford to pay very much. There is essentially no land development or construction going on.

Of increasing importance in blocking construction projects are the various rules passed in response to the demands of special-interest groups, which, in effect, assert that they have new rights in the private property of others. Some of the groups assert that they have a right that the countryside and even urban areas look the way they have in the past. This precludes a property owner from building a new structure or altering the landscape in some other way. Other special interests assert that their favored animals or plants have a right to use the land, especially rural land, and must be accommodated by the owner.

While it is difficult to make a reasonable return on investments in Comet Island, it is not difficult for those who have wealth to hang on to it even including their real estate. There have been episodes of substantial inflation and most people with money keep a good share of their savings in gold or valuable small artifacts or in foreign banks. However, at the moment the inflation is minimal. For those who know the game, the cost of living is not particularly high. Typically, it is the people on welfare who walk into the regular stores and pay full price for things. They can afford it. Their government allowances are calculated on that basis.

Most of the items that the island manufactured in the past can be made more cheaply in countries where the factories can legally pay lower wages. The vigorous part of the manufacturing economy on Comet Island is the small fly-by-night manufacturers, who use decrepit equipment to take advantage of transitory, fad markets in bigger countries. Along with breaking the labor rules, these companies are usually not in compliance with safety and waste-disposal regulations. The rules are not applied against them very often, but they are strictly applied against the few large companies that still have operations on the island.

Despite their own problems, nobody on Comet Island envies the NSS system anymore. After watching it for many decades, few Comet Islanders doubt that the NSS will always have a lower standard of living than their own. Compared to the NSS, Comet Island has also become very egalitarian. Nobody has servants, because nobody can afford to pay them as much as they can get on welfare.

The pace of life on Comet Island is relatively slow and the population is aging. Younger people who are ambitious try to emigrate to a more vigorous economy. The big fear that hangs over workers is that the economy, when they retire in a few more decades, will not be vigorous enough to provide for them. The government has promised that adequate provision will be made for all eligible citizens. Giving a reasonable interpretation to this promise, economists project this is not possible.

A visitor who comes to Comet Island would think it a little worn out. The chaotic jumble of bright-colored signs in the metropolitan area no longer makes the impression it once did. The colors are now faded and some of the the signs hang a little crooked. Neither commerce nor industry is very robust, compared to earlier days. Only the tourist industry has continued to function at near capacity.

16

Special-Interest-Group Democracy

With the signing of the social contract the people on Comet Island lived in a pure free society, a pioneer community in which people lived apart and largely interacted on a one-to-one basis. The island itself was isolated from the rest of the world. Only the first steps of the development were being taken. The brief set of rules appropriate to a free society reflected these factors.

Immigration increased, Comet Island reached a higher population density, and people interacted to a considerable extent in groups. The society had developed substantial contacts with other countries. These and other factors led to the constitution, followed by a more extensive set of legislated rules and a government. All this required that the society adopt a system of taxation—the first obligatory positive action required of all the members by the society.

In the years since then, the politicians have steered the government, step-by-step, deep into the everyday lives of its citizens. This started with a substantial and progressive expansion of taxes and other civic duties. Later the government branched out into rule systems that were aimed at benefiting specific groups of citizens. Finally, rules were added that singled out specific citizens to bear particular sacrifices.

These trends changed Comet Island in many ways: some visible, some embodied in the citizens' views of their rights.

CITIZENSHIP

By now, the memory of the inferior legal status of women in the early days of the Comet Island society is an embarrassment. The idea of the family as the basic membership unit had been forgotten and the constitution, as initially adopted, changed that by limiting official political activity and voting to men as individuals. Most people can't imagine that there ever was any reasonable justification for such a limitation, and no one would consider returning to it. Nevertheless, the subsequent change to equal rights for every person left children in a somewhat ambiguous legal position. In putting the old system behind them, the legislators made many speeches in support of the theory that every native-born person is a citizen and should have all the rights of a citizen, regardless of age or sex.

This may be fine for men and women, but children obviously need a substantial amount of support, protection, and discipline. The view that children are citizens leads the government to give them considerable, but as yet ill-defined, rights against their parents. On the other hand, when there is a rash of teenage gang violence, the government threatens action against parents who do not keep their children under control. It is also true that in child-custody proceedings the court places the child in the hands of some adult. Thus it is clear that, as a practical matter, children are not accorded all the rights of adults despite the theory. This is not a major problem, but it is one example that could be cited of actions by the Comet Island legislature showing a lack of understanding or, perhaps, lack of concern for the underlying theory of its political system.

In terms of the concepts proposed in this book, the citizens, children as well as adults, of a status society, such as the early one on Ajax Island, have all their rights directly against the society rather than against any individual. The rights of all individuals depend on their status, and the status of children is definitely affected by consideration of age.

In contrast, in the early Comet Island free society, children were not directly members of the society. Families were the recognized society membership units; individuals, including children, were members of families. In such a society the children are the responsibility of the family as a unit. The family both fulfills the obligations and exercises the rights. The family is a status society, at least in part, and internally it performs the functions of a primary status society.

Children are not suitable for full membership in a primary free society. Either the premise of full responsibility has to be changed, such as by the addition of appropriate status-society institutions and rules, or children should be given a status as something less than full members of society.

As a practical matter, children were not treated as full citizens on Comet Island, and society continued to hold the parents responsible in certain circumstances. In other circumstances children were treated as having the full rights of citizens. The courts handled this ambiguity by favoring the children, except in circumstances where that opposed the prevailing political sentiment.

As the Comet Island society grew more complicated, this same problem came up with regard to adults who were not capable of taking responsibility for themselves. Again, the conflict between their full rights as citizens and their need for care and support caused complications and required creative adjudication, all of which was done without facing the underlying theoretical problem.

It would seem that citizenship on Comet Island does not mean what membership did in either the status or the free society. Nor is one universal type of citizenship necessarily appropriate, given the range of behavior the government expects from its citizens. Perhaps there should be different categories of citizens with different legal implications in a welfare state. The choice of category could be voluntary in accordance with the underlying free-society system of rules.

WELFARE

The various welfare programs on Comet Island were originally an expression of charitable feelings evoked by the plight of people in unfortunate circumstances. The voters expected the welfare recipients to react as the voters imagined they themselves would, and assumed that the payments would be temporary. However, as the decades wore on, there were more and more long-term welfare recipients, including some adults who had been raised in homes supported by welfare. Many voters thought some of the recipients were taking advantage of the system to avoid work. They viewed welfare recipients as a permanent underclass and many citizens ceased to be sympathetic.

The record suggested that the welfare system provided a modest standard of living for recipients but was not successful in upgrading them to become self-supporting citizens. Worse, the welfare system seemed particularly deficient in sponsoring the raising of children to become responsible and productive adults. It annoyed voters that they were paying taxes to support people they did not approve of and they pressed to make sure the welfare recipients did not squander the money. Those who received welfare asserted their rights to free choice as citizens. The upshot was a welfare system that was costly to the taxpayers and utilized a sizable bureaucracy, but was niggardly in its treatment of the individual welfare recipients and showed meager accomplishments. Nobody was pleased.

In terms of the approach being described here, the functions of a welfare system can be viewed as derived from (1) mandatory insurance, or (2) the distribution function of a primary status society. The insurance function applies to people who are handicapped in some way but are still capable of being responsible, perhaps with financial assistance, for their own lives. In such cases, if the handicap is cured or surmounted, the recipients would presumably resume full responsibility for themselves. The distribution function, on the other hand, applies to people who need continuing support because they are fundamentally not capable of taking full responsibility for themselves.

The insurance class of welfare recipients includes those who were taking adequate care of themselves and their families until they became unable to do so. This might have been due to the death of a principal wage earner in the family, medical disabilities, economic setbacks, or whatever. Many of the recipients in this class need only short-term welfare payments. The important point is that even those in this class who are permanently physically disabled are capable of assuming responsibility for themselves, given financial or medical assistance. Orphaned children are in this class and are expected to take full responsibility for themselves when they are grown.

In these cases, the welfare system functions as though it were a compulsory form of insurance. The benefit of having this insurance is uniform across the population. As with any form of insurance, the payout, a consequence of this benefit, is to those who qualify through some involuntary event. Since the benefit is uniform, it should not have an adverse effect on the functioning of the free-society network of rules, apart from the related tax payments.

There is another type of welfare recipient: those persons who are not capable of taking responsibility for themselves even when they have the financial and physical assets to do so. Helping such people by giving them financial and medical assistance does not solve the problem. They need another dimension of support, i.e., somebody to tell them what to do, and, if necessary, require them to do it. Such support is included in that provided by the distribution function of a status society.

These welfare recipients may be mentally or emotionally deficient. They may come from a cultural background so at odds with the free society that they cannot learn to function in it. They may be addicted to drugs, alcohol, or something else to the extent that it supersedes their will to do what they know is best. These recipients may have demonstrated by criminal behavior that they do not choose to behave in a lawful manner. Such people may need help to forestall harm to themselves and to the rest of society. In any case, such people need assistance that is tailored to their particular problems—the type of assistance they would get in a status society—a major element of which is compulsory supervision. This does not fit with free-society ethical principles and is traditionally not used by hybrid free societies, except in prisons, where there is no attempt to provide prisoners with full citizen's rights.

In welfare assistance, the insurance cases should be distinguished from the status-society support cases. The former can be handled within the framework of hybrid free-society rules. The status-society support cases might best be handled by taking care of recipients in a subsociety, an institution run on status-society terms. If done, this should be for the welfare of the clients and there should not be elements of punishment or implications that such an institution is unpleasant.

In treating welfare recipients, there is apt to be an implicit assumption that they could be responsible for themselves and their children if they just had a financial boost to get them started. If this assumption turns out to be wrong—for particular persons or an entire class of welfare recipients—there should be a shift from insurance to status-society distribution-type treatment. What is at stake is more than the money that is spent, more than the effects on the morale of the rest of the population. It is the children who may be ruined by irresponsible parents who assert their right to raise them as a way of getting welfare payments. Whatever the government does, it has the obligation to its citizens to do its best. If it undertakes a status-society relationship, as it does with welfare recipients, it ought to discharge this obligation to the children ahead of anybody else because their need is greater. In practical terms this requires a mechanism to be developed that will raise the children to be self-supporting, responsible adults.

TAXES

Taxes in the hybrid free society are not a major problem because they do not amount to much. The welfare society, in contrast, needs far more money and raises taxes to much higher levels in order to finance the much higher level of benefits it provides.

The fact that legislators find they can get elected by voting for benefits certainly doesn't retard the trend toward adding more and more benefits. Of course, legislators also try to avoid angering their constituents with heavier tax burdens. This leads representatives to tax affluent minorities through such mechanisms as progressive rates. However, since the free society is a market society, people who are taxed will act to minimize the effect of the tax, and in doing so will affect the overall economy. Very high tax rates can cause substantial degradation of the economy, thereby leading to major productivity declines and resulting in continuing conflict between the pressures for more governmental benefits and for strengthening the market economy.

Taxes are a status-society feature and a classical use of the positive rule. When taxes are added to a society that has a foundation of free-society rules, interference with the foundation rules is minimized if taxes are applied uniformly to everyone. On the face of it, a detriment, such as a tax, is best applied if it is proportional to assets that (1) can be most easily evaluated in terms of money, (2) bring in the most money to the taxpayers, and (3) are the most highly regarded by taxpayers. Time and possessions suggest themselves. A uniform tax assessment would be the same proportion of the product of each citizen's time (perhaps income) and the same proportion of each citizen's property.

One can impose taxes for more reasons than merely to raise money. In the status society, the required contribution from a member is likely to serve several purposes. In the welfare society, too, taxes are configured for purposes such as penalizing the wealthy, penalizing members who sin, and other purposes that have little to do with raising tax money. Such nonuniform taxes interfere in various ways with the operation of the underlying free society. These taxes usually involve designating classes of members: a normal activity in the status society, but one that the free society is not equipped to do properly. Classification of members by status is not in accordance with the principles of the free society, in which all rules are applied the same way to everyone—a one-class society, so to speak. The welfare society, being fundamentally a form of free society, usually has only a part of the mechanism needed to classify people accurately in terms that are relevant to the purpose of the classification.

In the welfare state, the legislature usually designates such classifications, even though they are not in accordance with free-society principles and the legislature is not a suitable mechanism for making them. Legislators are inherently motivated by the benefits they are able to provide their constituents. In a free society the partisan approach is counterbalanced by the overriding principle that rules apply the same to all members, which would preclude status classifications. Legislative classification is not in accordance with status-society principles either, because the status society abhors partisan decisions.

This principle has a broader application. The legislature of a welfare state, as long as it operates in a partisan manner as though it were part of a free society, should restrict itself, when making status-society-type rules, to those that establish a general function or set funding priorities. For example, a legislature might appropriately determine how much of the budget should be spent on transportation. It is not in accordance with either free-society or status-society principles for the legislature to rule that a particular bridge be built. It is also not an appropriate legislative function to single out a particular group to be taxed or excluded from taxation.

If status is to be introduced in a modified free society, the managers of the government departments should be the ones to make the detailed decisions on the classifications or the assignment of particular people or situations to classes. As in the status society, they should function on a strictly impartial basis for the good of the whole society.

Unfortunately, people are frequently deeply cynical about whether the managers will make the correct decisions. This attitude often reflects a well-deserved lack of respect for the managers. To the extent that a modified free society insists on status-society rules requiring the assignment of members to classes, then it is important that the society locate managers who have the analytical skills needed to make clearly better decisions, in this area of expertise, than can the rest of the population. Of course it is also vital that the managers avoid letting personal motives affect their decisions, as they would if they were in a primary status society.

SPECIAL BENEFITS FOR SPECIAL GROUPS

Groups seeking special benefits for themselves are a standard feature of partisan politics in legislatures. Where the legislators are elected by geographical districts, people in a specific district seek local improvements of roads and other infrastructure, new local-government services, special assistance for local-government institutions such as schools, and so on. The voters may even elect their legislators based on promises to secure such benefits.

These actions may benefit the local district differentially when only a few districts receive such benefits. When most of the districts demand special benefits, the legislators have to see that all of them receive something. To do this, the legislators must add a layer of expenditure above the normal cost of government. This has all the bad (but none of the good) features of a round of gift giving. Everyone must pay for the gifts, plus the cost of administering the system, but each district gets, at best, what is available at the time or what the legislature thinks the district might settle for.

In due course, groups other than those geographically attached to a particular legislator will seek special benefits, too. Benefits for such groups are generally positive and go directly to individuals since the groups are often not in a position to benefit differentially to the rest of the society from a social good. Such individual benefits may be special treatment for members of the group, e.g., preference for certain jobs, promotions, supply contracts, enrollment in prestigious schools, and so forth. One problem with giving preferences is that for every person benefited, someone else suffers a detriment.

More problems arise when the preferences are justified on the basis of compensating for a lack of ability. An agency or school that gives preferences instead of choosing on the basis of merit will be perceived by the public as tolerating a lower quality of performance from members of the preferred group. The existence of preferences also denigrates the accomplishments of the members of the special group, something particularly galling to those who would have achieved without the preferences.

Again, as in the case of geographically oriented benefits, the success of one special-interest group prompts others to seek benefits, too. In due course, there will be many special-interest groups competing for the same preferences. Such a contest makes a mockery of the merit system that stands as a fundamental ethical principle of the status society. Interference with private activities on such a basis clearly violates free-society principles also.

The preferences are of the status-society type, but the classification required is not in accordance with status-society principles. In the welfare system, individual recipients qualify as members of the privileged class by possessing the characteristics that the benefits are intended to remedy. In the case of special-interest-group classifications, this is not the case. Members of special-interest groups qualify for the class by religion, skin color, ethnic background, or whatever else is in vogue. The benefits have no necessary connection with these "criteria."

In place of a necessary connection, it is customary to claim that there is a statistical connection. The argument is that members of the class deserve a benefit because a larger proportion of them is thought to need it than the rest of the population. Obviously, this is a tenuous connection. In operation, it comes close to presuming that giving the benefit to members of the class who don't need it is as good as giving it to those who do and better than giving it to those who need it but are not members of the class.

This special-interest-group approach does not satisfy the ethical principles of either the free or status society. The rules do not produce uniform benefits. They do not reflect an attempt to tailor benefits to the needs of individual members of the society.

SPECIAL DETRIMENTS FOR SPECIAL GROUPS

In general, in societies having a foundation of free-society rules, the members expect equal treatment under the rules in the free-society sense. People notice even minute variations when they are treated differently from others, either in terms of benefits or detriments.

The members of free societies build their lives around property rights—the right to their own minds and bodies as well as to their other possessions. Broadly speaking, property encompasses the resources that people have at their command to achieve their goals.

At the same time, even hybrid free-society members would concede that there may be occasions when society's need for property outweighs the owner's claim to it. They understand that it may be appropriate for society to take the property provided that the owner is in some way placed in an equivalent new position. Payment of the full value is one way this can be done in some cases.

As welfare societies evolve, there is a tendency for the government to contribute progressively more and more benefits to the members. One might fear that the government would commit all the money it can conveniently raise by taxation, inflation, and external loans until its resources run out. The situation is worse than this: special-interest groups continue to demand more benefits, and some governments will look for ways to satisfy the requests by the use of the resources of individual citizens who happen to fall into specific groups.

One approach is to require that citizens who happen to own particular kinds of property suffer the detriment. This is done, for example, when using price controls, rent controls, land-use restrictions, required public easements, and the like. Sometimes the taking of property rights is accomplished using ostensibly negative rules that do not on their face seem to constitute property seizure. For example, the rule might say that a citizen cannot sell or rent something for greater than a certain price. In some cases the rule goes beyond this and says that the owner must continue to rent the property at the same set price. In any case, the rules have the effect of allocating the victim's property or its value to someone else's use.

This mechanism involves changing the rules in the middle of the game, which violates a very fundamental free-society ethical principle. A person invests in an apartment building, and a few days later the government requires not only that it be rented but sets the rent that can be charged. The owner thereby loses some of the use of the property. In due course, price control very often results in a shortage of the controlled product. For example, experience has shown that in cases where rent-control regulations are strict and economically binding, the result may be deterioration of whole neighborhoods, until finally an uninhabitable wasteland results. The effects on the society, however, extend much further. People avoid investments they fear might catch the eye of the legislature, investing instead in things they can conceal.

Another effect of such rules is to stimulate people to keep their property out of the reach of foreseeable rules. In current examples, owners who suspect they might have an endangered species on their land, or that someone might view their house as a historic monument, sometimes take preventive action by clearing the land or renovating the house so that their neighbors will lose interest.

In terms of free-society and status-society principles, the benefits with this kind of rule may be presumed to be general and often of the nature of social goods. This presumption is frequently incorrect; there is a special-interest beneficiary group as well as a special-interest detriment involved. The detriment, however, is quite specific and individual. Neither status- nor free-society principles permit individuals to be singled out for such sacrifices unless there is some overwhelming necessity. Civilizations that practiced human sacrifice did something that formally resembled these special-interest detriments, but such civilizations had the excuse that human life can only be contributed on an individual basis. In the modern special-interest group version of such practices, the detriment is generally economic and could well be borne by the whole society through taxation or assessment. While the purpose of some of these activities may be laudable, it is difficult to defend the means used to pay for them, or to overestimate the long-range damage they can do to the free-society elements that remain.

17

Remarks

THE ILLUSTRATIONS

Most of the features of the fictitious societies in the story of the Tidy Isles have been copied from real life, and I trust the descriptions are plausible, i.e., that these societies could have came about. But the examples are not intended to be a claim that this is the way such societies would normally develop, nor that, historically, this is the way they did develop in some particular place, nor certainly that there is any reason to say that they should develop this way. The examples were designed to illustrate the political theory.

However, in describing a pure free society and a pure status society, I did make an attempt to picture each of these societies favorably. This was not intended to give the reader the impression that comparing these two societies would support a useful conclusion about their relative value. Rather, using favorable examples was meant to suggest conditions that are needed to produce a satisfactory society with each of the two approaches. Absence of some of the conditions would be expected to lead to the introduction of opposite-type rules to improve the situation.

This is not to say that I am lacking in opinions about the type of rules that would be best for a state, or that I would pass up the opportunity to mention them. But I should admit that these opinions are based on impressions from travel and reading the news rather than on the results of a proper study of these matters.

THE INDIGENOUS SOCIETY

My perception of the degree to which people appreciate their government is based on my impression of their desire to emigrate, immigrate, or stay put, and how strongly they appear to feel about it. It is not hard to conclude that people in many states are not pleased with the way their respective rules and governments function. By now it has become clear that big government is not an effective tool for directly handling any broad range of economic activities. This is to say that government operation of the means of production, distribution, or the link between the two has been an almost universal failure by modern standards. Since these have been features of Marxist societies, the Marxist models of government are being widely discarded.

Many current forms of dictatorship—African, Hispanic-American, and others—are also unpopular, probably stemming from the government actions that are directed primarily to support the well-being and favorite ideas of the rulers rather than to benefit the general population. There are various advanced European-type socialist states that also seem to be losing popularity as the years go by.

However, there do appear to be two rather different kinds of modern states that have the potential to provide a satisfactory life for their citizens. The first of these I will call "indigenous societies," the second "melting pot societies."

Quite a variety of societies can be classified as indigenous. They are nations in the classical sense of a people who share a culture distinct from that of their neighbors and who have a well-developed sense of nationhood. Two years ago, I spent a few days in Caucasian Georgia and got the strong impression that it was an indigenous society. The Georgians have their own language, both written and oral, a couple of millennia during which they occupied the same land, a common religion, and many shared cultural practices and attitudes, all of which bind them together.

There are many other such indigenous societies in a wide range of cultures; typically they have a considerable degree of cultural homogeneity. These states are often not very tolerant of permanent residents who do not practice the dominant culture within their borders. In fact, acting in accordance with the culture appears to be of higher priority to the society than individuals' satisfying their own personal choices.

Basically these indigenous societies appear to be heavily modified forms of status societies. There is a basic requirement that all citizens do their part to carry on the culture. Fortunately, the cultures frequently incorporate centuries of empirical knowledge about how to live a satisfying life and run a state successfully, and most natives seem to be quite happy to live in such cultures.

In many of these societies the actions required to conform to the culture take only a small amount of time. Thereafter, members of the society are free to act in pursuit of economic benefits or any other legitimate interests, including art, science, and scholarship. Often the requirements of the culture do not interfere with such activities and may indeed provide a favorable environment.

Thus, encapsulated within a status-society framework may be a large, viable, free-society zone, available to all citizens, although the free-society approach is probably not permitted to extend into all aspects of societal life. Japan, a very large and complicated society, may be in essence an indigenous society, and a particularly powerful and successful one.

Such societies are not without their problems. In the case of Georgia there are at least two enclaves, the Ossetians and Abkhazinians, that are themselves indigenous societies. One of the questions that comes up in many cases is this: How small can an indigenous society be and still function adequately as a primary society?

An even more difficult problem occurs when two indigenous societies occupy the same land. The heart of the indigenous society is its homogeneous culture. It does not appear to be feasible to impose two independent compulsory cultures on different peoples who happen to live intermixed in the same area. As mentioned earlier, there can only be one primary society in an area. The problem is illustrated in Israel and South Africa. In both cases the modern world rejects the idea that the dominant culture be allowed to accommodate the intermixture by use of a caste system.

At the same time there is nothing I know of to suggest that two unrelated cultures can be merged as equals in a way that satisfies both peoples. The practical alternatives appear to be (1) the destruction of one of the cultures and conversion of its adherents to the surviving culture, perhaps with retention of some of the rejected culture's features, as has happened often in the history of the world and fairly recently in the freed colonies of Africa; (2) ejection of one of the peoples and their culture, as occurred in the United States during its settlement by Europeans and has been going on in Israel; or (3) the partition of the land between cultural groups, as was done in India.

Over the last several centuries, a large number of these indigenous societies were incorporated into larger states, often as separate provinces. The driving force was usually the imperial ambitions of the dominant state, but it could have been argued that small independent states could not defend themselves and could not reach the minimum critical mass for a healthy economy. These reasons have been and are disappearing.

As regards imperial ambitions, most modern states have concluded that annexing a foreign state with an indigenous culture is not desirable, unless of course, it has large oil reserves or some equivalent asset. In addition, the world seems to have become less tolerant of naked aggression across international boundaries. With the thawing of the cold war and the example of the international police action against Iraq, one might hope that this problem will not stand in the way of independence for small indigenous societies.

In the modern world, some small states have prospered economically as much as large ones in favorable cases. Singapore and Switzerland are prime examples. Apparently the size of the state is not a critical factor; rather, the limits on economic performance seem to be related more to the actions of the government.

Currently Soviet Georgia is embarked on a course that would ultimately sever its ties with Moscow, Croatia is doing the same in Yugoslavia, and similar action is under consideration in Quebec. There are many other indigenous societies where there has been agitation for separation: for example, the Kurds and the Basques. Not all of these societies have an opportunity to govern themselves. Such separatist movements are resisted by the central governments of states where they take place, and even in countries such as the United States, which have no real problems of this sort, there is a lack of sympathy stemming from ignorance. Here also, unfortunately, there is a tendency to think that we have some special knowledge of the only worthwhile way to organize a state for all peoples. The idea of a number of small indigenous states, each with its own culture, conflicts with that vision.

Consider how Ajax Island could have become a successful indigenous society. The people could have decided that the only important thing was the two-hour philosophy discussions each day. If they had required this, but left the economic and social activities to be conducted under free-society rules, a private enterprise economy and lifestyle would have sprung up like a crop of weeds in the unoccupied parts of the Ajax Island culture. The result might have been something like a religious state, perhaps akin to Israel, or a good Moslem or Catholic state. Of course, other mechanisms could have led them to other types of indigenous societies.

The indigenous state can provide a good life for citizens who like the culture, but the society needs to be homogeneous, stable, reasonably equitable, and must provide for a free-enterprise economy. These factors are much easier to work out if the state is relatively small.

THE MELTING POT

The other favored form of society, the melting-pot society, has a quite different set of characteristics and mode of operation. It is a society constantly in flux: individuals are not tied to any particular culture but are free to affiliate with one of their choice or to pick and choose their own menu of personal cultural practices, so long as they accord their neighbors the same opportunity. Such a society has a heterogeneous mixture of cultures, some imported from other societies, others created by the inhabitants.

The United States has been a traditional example of such a state, although an example marred by various compulsory cultural features. People in the United States are very mobile (e.g., those who live in Los Angeles move, on the average, every four years) and it is relatively un-common to have families occupy a piece of land for multiple generations. There is a common language for legally required communications and for practical purposes, but no particular legal barrier to the use of any language the citizens wish to use between themselves.

The melting pot clearly calls for a free-society foundation. In place of the cultural support provided by the indigenous societies, there is freedom to do whatever one wants. While the indigenous society displays a certain amount of rigidity and solidity, the melting pot is fundamentally liquid. Just as there can be many configurations of solids, there can be many desirable kinds of status societies. On the other hand, as a first approxi-mation, there is only one liquid state and essentially only one desirable kind of melting-pot society.

Unlike the indigenous society, the melting pot works better as it gets bigger. Much of its strength lies in the opportunities that can be found by its citizens. The bigger the state the bigger the variety of contacts, of geographical area, of potentially congenial neighbors. A big melting-pot state supports a big free-enterprise economy, including a large market with many nooks and crannies to match the individual needs, tastes, and interests of the population.

While a big melting-pot state is well-suited to free-society features, it is not particularly appropriate as a platform on which to mount status-society institutions. The melting pot, like nature, is made up of numerous disparate elements, each going its own way. Its elements, if permitted to operate freely and naturally, will wear down, upset, outflank, and in various ways mistreat status-society features, just as nature degrades the physical structures built by humans. When the government attempts to change the character of the melting-pot society to make it more hospitable to status-society features the free-society elements are damaged. As has been discussed earlier, some types of status-society provisions are more damaging to free-society operations than others. The worst are rules that strike at the long-range predictability of private economic or other personal commitments.

As has been suggested earlier, the best approach to the problem seems to be to insulate the damaging parts of the status-society institutions from the free society. This is not so different from the solution that successful indigenous societies use to combine a free-society feature into their status society. In that case, too, the status-society elements are kept separated from the free-society function.

The free-enterprise system in the United States has been very productive and has shown great vigor. But it is being eaten away, piece by piece, by laws and regulations made to benefit pressure groups. The extent of the damage may not be known for quite a while, because much of it is reflected in actions not taken. Increasingly people are dissuaded from taking economic risks, for example, because these risks are multiplied unreasonably by partisan regulations.

The legislature is properly partisan in a free society, but this factor should be balanced by a reluctance on the part of the legislature to involve itself in the details of status-society activities. The executive and judicial branches at all levels should not be partisan. The present system has moved so far from these ideals that a great many citizens assume that the government is inherently corrupt. This leads much of the population to involve itself only when it has to, with distaste, to protect itself from government actions or to get some of the spoils.

The hybrid free society, which seems to be approximately the vision of the libertarians, is well-suited to the melting pot. The closer such a society can get to this, the better it should work.

CONCLUSION

The starting point of this political theory has been the postulate that the actions people choose to initiate are purposeful. The heart of the theory is the assertion that when people coordinate their choice of actions with each other in the light of their purposes, they necessarily take one or both of two approaches. One is to share a purpose and coordinate choices to that end. The other is to retain individual purposes and coordinate choices to avoid interfering with each other.

This book has presented definitions related to and deductions derived from this concept. Where there is no coordination, we do not have a society. Where there is coordination of the first type only, the result will be a status society; of the second type only, a free society. It is hoped that the explanations and illustrations will encourage the reader to apply the political theory to situations of everyday life.